Odd bent

Coppers

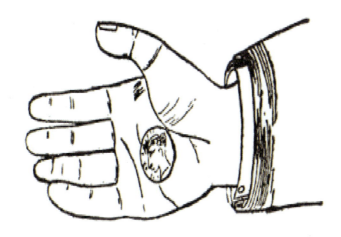

Copyright AG Enterprises 2016

2nd Edition February 2nd

www.landrucuchulainstarword.co.uk

<u>Home</u>

Welcome to one of the most unusual and intriguing sites on the net.

The *Literature* section comprises a number of different *HIVES* each containing a selection of short stories, poems, and <u>political satire.</u>

There is also a section involving **Prophecy** and **Prediction**, **Spells** and **Invocations**.

You can also order your own personalised **ASBO.**

I have long considered writing to be a *form of art*. The Artwork section contains pages from the *infamous* 'THUNDERBUCK RAM.'

BELINDA'S HOT AIR gives participants of the site the opportunity to express their views on a very diverse range of subjects. By clicking on the heading you can add your own comments, but you need to be signed in to *Facebook.*

FIRST CONTACT is a forum for new untested art forms and experimental writing.

> **In an age of increasing state control and monitoring your general comments and feedback are positively encouraged.**
> **Our freedom of speech and liberal values have to be permanently fought for or else they are lost.**

Live dangerously and to your heart be true.

Proxima Centauri Alpha
L0+4A

INTRODUCTION

After fleeing to Ireland in search of a better life I returned to the heath moor above Aylsham pursued by the fuzz. It is a land frequented by rabbits and the occasional deer. Snakes are reputed to strike without warning in the nearby woods. I have been visited by fairies. I'm a little reluctant to go out at night if I can hear sniffing outside my window. On my fateful Cannondale I have been disturbed by the occasional horse-rider and a massive Rottweiler leading a small dwarf-like woman. I don't know what the future holds. I have been known to rise from the ashes before. All I could see was a black fog blotting out the Sun and dark clouds rising in the morning. Burning of the Scarlet Hearts

READERS

ARE INVITED TO MAKE THEIR COMMENTS

THROUGHOUT

WITHOUT OBSCURING THE ORIGINAL

TEXT

Sign and date ALL your remarks and insults

GUDRUN BUNDERCHOOK

www.landrucuchulainstarword.co.uk

Contents

Power and utility not bad, aggression a necessity

By Usuli Twelves | Published: May 14, 2015 | Edit

Why do Governments always pretend that power is bad (unless it's in *their* hands of course) and that it is wrong for people to use each other?

What is the point in trying to legislate against the *facts of life* (unless you suffer from the 'do-gooder' syndrome)?

Truth is not so feeble a creature that it will ever be suppressed by the laws of the ignorant.

Poison

By Usuli Twelves | Published: May 17, 2015 | Edit

Dear P-in-the-bum,

I think mum might be trying to poison me. I saw her placing one of her prescription drugs in my sandwich.

She's determined to stop me writing at all costs!

Elderly parent health report

By Godfrey Winklebacker | Published: May 11, 2015 | Edit

Dear pain-in-the-butt,

Mum is showing increasing signs of:

1 Disturbed and irritable behaviour

2 Sleep walking, mumbling and incoherent speech

3 Sudden and inexplicable changes of mood

4 Irrational and emotional outbursts

5 Hiding things so we can't find them

6 Rages, accusations and general mayhem

7 Lying, trickery and subterfuge

* Pretty much as **normal** then.

NB I don't wish to alarm you but the sound of plates being smashed in the kitchen at night is very alarming and she wants to know what you have done with her bread knife.

PRETTY BABY

Beneath Buckhurst hill, whose cobbled texture,
known by locals as the *Anaconda*, drawn like a
draughtsman's stroke from another place upon the
earthly gradient, wound its way down from
Rombald's summit, where a ghostly army sometimes
trod across the desolate moors in winter, passing
a primeval quarry of red brick along the route,
slithering between a series of undulating burial
mounds, and an old straight track leading to a
hive of dilapidated buildings over-grown with an
orgy of blackberry thickets, until the Incalike
scales, shining with an ochreous skin, petered-out
in the lower reaches, at the second row of quaint
stone cottages above the farmhouse.

A trail of snuff dribbled from one of those
monstrous chimney stacks over the ancient valley
to Riddlesden. The spandrel finally crept by
Walls Shipping, where the reptile secreted its
sebaceous fluid, overlooking the nearby coal yard,
and Ramsden lymph towers beyond the croft, before
laying its gleaming fangs in the line of sullen
tinker trucks at the bottom: constantly being
harassed to move on.

The snake, like a prowling *cthonian* spirit
lying in wait for the tribe of young innocents,
who pranced across the big green field in summer,
carrying their jam-jars of newts and tadpoles,
from the small pond perched in the dip, below the
third wooden copse in the hill's mist.

Like a plethora of tiny unleavened copings with
their diary of woollen weeds vermiculating their
crammed cracks, which suddenly awoke erect to the
piercing scream of a woman's fraught voice, just
as the streak steamed under the railway bridge at
the nadir of the knife edge.

5

The distant hum of the chemical works still clogged the discordant sky with a torch of tyrant flame. He'd been chased the previous night for pedalling blindfold.

The pedlar persevered towards the buckler where the fauna unfolded like a sodden *garden of Eden*.

Shaking his dice in a pint-gallon cup he flung them against the violent sea of spray.

His darkroom timer began to fright as he ploughed along the old straight track with the wind beating fiercely agin im. Whims of the not so young.

The yellow lantern glimmered weakly through the *Cider Wood* as he fought bravely against the baser elements, drawing him like a magnet towards the cove of Stamford.

He navigated the *oar-scull* where the mute swans had taken refuge in the banking, and a Barn Owl suddenly appearing in the branch above him had made his heart beat much faster then.

The stellar motion gleamed like mica overhead as chalkdust nodded to its fall through the glass bottle recently shaken...

Our wayfarer approached the spinney gate with his head swimming, below the rising moon coruscating on the silver ripples of the horse-shoe bend.

The raven shadow of a silent punt bubbled like a barm of thistle down through the clutching mist with its ghostly troupe of randan fugitives.

A small trail of mustard gas crooned from the summit of Neptune's chimney as he picked his way through the bare blackberry bushes teeming in the ether.

Just as he was equating the hedgerow to hog the wooden rampart F.'s bicycle chain snapped with a 'twang' of *feu de joie*...the cyclist jogged the last few yards over the gravel bed with the contraption under his arm.

He hesitated by the coal bunker to rip-off the plastic bin-liners ensconced with rubber bands, and clanked over the cinders to call on his relief still bantering on the telephone at the top, and filled with profligate vitriol.

116

Dazed and confused the glazed eyes of the 'Elephant Girl' dilated to two diminishing pin-holes.

She withdrew her grasp and hung her head in shame while he finished paddling his own canoe.

"I don't know what you want me to do!" she bleated.

"I suppose you want to go to sleep now?" she extrapolated...

F. thought that he heard the succinct rattle of his downstairs postbox. He ventured gingerly forth to moot this bolt from the blue.

An arrow-head had been hastily drawn...'Love Vivienne, X.'

109

While the union *untouchable* crept for his two hour *charr wallah* F. was required to empty all the waste paper bins with his yellow dust cart.

He flushed and tried to hide his face from view of the general public. Bit of skirt. Red-alert! He was commanded to attend all manner of ordured chores while the red carpet was rolled out for the approaching contact of a *feudal monarch*.

For an eternity the Flash laboured solidly at a stretch of ordinary wall with a brand of fluid named in his honour.

Then he was ordered to *fluff* down the buffer stops resurrecting in the hot rays of the sun.

With Balzac's hands the *shit-picker* collected in his trade of satiated condoms and oily crisp packets, re-gurgitated disembogue and canine crap.

A large swarm of Caddis scorched along the black bum of the corridoor and followed his stinking carcass across the blades. On reflection a swat would have been expedient. Clogged-up leafs of Seabrooke packs!

In a secluded hold beneath the overhang a family of vermin gathered overhead to make crude insinuations. F. asked permission to pay a visit to the pit. The epaulettes of his jacket were soon covered in *monkey spit*. His Hornby train set off.

"Are you a blinking warptwister? Do it down there you mucky sod," grinned O'Flanagan. No way!

"It's never stopped you having a wank in the open air before. Take a good look at his face everyone!"

He emptied a container of used tickets over his bald acropolis. Turd found in a milk bottle.

When F. severed his links to avoid further humiliation the Supervisor tracked him down after a few brief seconds in the locker room.

"If I ever catch you shirking once more!" he screamed, "you're on your bike ya mucky little cunt." And so it was! "Keep your hair on, Baldy!"

'Eat shit!' A billion blackflies can't be wrong,' F. sighed. Get thee forth and multiply.

"Do you have 'fly-fishing,' by J.R.R. Hartley?"

228

His heart was beating wildly as he trotted down the steps towards the taxi ranks with an anxious backward glance. He could procrastinate no longer. There but for the grace of god. Wordsmith, Swordsmith, no 's.'

Was it a 'love letter?' A phone number perhaps, or some words of gratitude and admiration?

Sneaking from the clouded recess beside the town hall clock the scarlet pimple poured out the *insider dealing* beneath the street lamp.

'YOU ARE PATHETIC, AND A DISGRACE TO SOCIETY!'

Placing the draft back into his pocket F. forced a toxic laugh, and sniggered. Another satisfied customer and completely *free of charge*! Once again he'd slid through the net. Gave her the iron heel.

Reaching for his Filofax the *bon enfant* decided to make a declaration to the S.S. warden, who had been specially allocated to *buddy* members of his group. The *Silent call*. Quite like J.'s policy of appeasement.

"I'm so sorry to trouble you on a Sunday," he salvoed. "I haven't rung you before because I thought you might be busy. You did say that we could contact you at any time of the night or day if we ever had any *little worries*."

'Call me 'Aunty Sheelagh' responded with the perfunctory zeal and surface sodality.

"That's alright lovey," she replied. "What's wrong? Would you like to tell me all about it?"

F. was about to tell her about the pressure he was feeling under at work when she interupted him...

"Oh, I am awfully sorry dearie," she white-washed. "But to be absolutely frank..."

Another big porky on its waythought F. Just like the P.M. All the books on topping yourself had been taken out and not returned.

"I can't spare the time to have a natter just now. I'm expecting a very important telephone call this evening from my son who is away at University. You'll be buggering up the line."

218

Female flashers

By [Adumla](#) | Published: July 29, 2015

I was walking down the main street in a lovely English village a few years ago when I saw something which greatly distressed me, and which I will never ever forget. I've been having nightmares about it ever since and my doctor is very worried in case I do something terrible. As I glanced across the street to the nearby telephone kiosk I saw a few local teenagers passing along the line of Residential properties.   I believe they lived on the same street. It was summertime.   I'd called in the church hall at the nearby farm estate and was making my way back home for tea. I could see a young woman among the group of about fifteen. She was quite buxom if I recall and had a rosy complexion. To my surprise she dropped her jeans and exposed herself. Quite frankly, I was shocked. She laughed and pulled them up again. I think she may even have blushed.   I was sick to my stomach and ran all the way home in case she attacked me to phone the Smeg-heads.

COMMENTS

Edward Heath in Kids company

By [Rumplestiltskin](#) | Published: August 5, 2015

The cat is finally out of the bag.   This Tory Government will do anything to win votes and suck up to Charities with a long record of incompetence. I suppose it would be a complete waste of time asking for a list of sponsors and how much money they donated?

If only Edward Heath were alive today. He seems to be very popular all of a sudden. The last I heard there were not three but five police forces racing to dig up his remains.

I don't quite understand why they keep saying he went to a brothel (euphemistically known as a *massage parlour*):

1 It's not actually against the law.

2 I thought *most* MP's went there once in a while.

"It's like this your Majesty: *guilty until proved innocent*!"

"I hear one of Janner's 'victims' is suffering from Cecil Parkinson's."

COMMENTS

Veronica

by

Gillie Mairtean

September 1996

*'I see first love in bloom upon your flesh,
dark or luminous I see your vanished days,
my teeming heart exults in all your sins,
and all your virtues magnify my soul.'*

'Baudelaire'

When I first arrived at Brookevale it was summertime and the garden was in full bloom.

It was a large Victorian building in a once proud area of the city.

I walked up the steep sides of Hem Lane as I had done twenty years before, on my way to the reputable Catholic Grammar school at the summit, where I had failed to gain a place at Oxford even though it had been expected of me. Burnt sienna and blushing schoolboy, painfully aware...

I turned left into the drive and ventured up the path towards the entrance.

I rang the bell and stood back to look up at the windows.

The paintwork was worn to a frazzle and the door dog-eared and dingy: not what I had been used to at the Trust, with its refurbished day-centres and high profile medals of honour for the management.

We sat down in the basement office alongside the Resident's filing cabinets.

I went pedantically through my life history, missing out all the controversial bits.

He said I was miles over-qualified but I convinced him I needed greater *job satisfaction.*

"I've always been interested in states-of-mind," I confessed.

I sat at the table in the worn-out dining room filling in my application form with a Biro that had seen better days.

A lady came to stand at the tea-boiler in front of me.

I thought she was dressed very conservatively. I wondered what her face was like.

Our eyes didn't meet even when she swished around and left the room. Thirty something?

My fingers tapped nervously on the table.

Daniel still seemed very keen, even when I told him why I had left my last post.

The new manager had only been there a week himself.

For some reason the Owner had trouble recruiting reliable staff.

I wasn't sure where my future lay but I was willing to give it a try.

Stephen usually had a room to himself on the ground floor. Gerald sometimes came to share with him, only to return home to his wife after one or two weeks of respite.

He was one of the night-owls who occupied the cane sofa in the porch trying to smoke himself into an early grave. He often spoke about his imminent death. His wife had just died of lung cancer.

Stephen said that he had never been himself since a man had tried to kiss him in a public lavatory when he was just fourteen. He was now in his early sixties and suffering from angina.

Next to him in the annex was Gilbert. Gilbert was nicknamed 'Taff' for some strange reason...

He'd had his head crushed by a steamroller one night on his way back from a tavern.

A section of his head was completely absent. He combed his hair like a peacock fan over the missing portion.

Gilbert liked to crack a joke or two, usually at someone else's expense.

Gilbert was always coughing up his guts, which made Stephen extremely angry.

If Stephen entered the dining room Gilbert would leave at once, and vice-versa.

Beside Gilbert resided Sam.

He'd once had a job in the laundry, and I think they had found him some work digging in the cemetery some time back, but that was years ago, before any of them moved out.

I think it was called 'community rehabilitation' or something like that...

Sam had a black tongue of leather incruscated with barnacles.

He looked like an old sea-captain, was unsteady on his pegs, and as gentle as a lamb.

On the first floor slept *Yousef* and *Madan*.

Most of the time their dwelling was like a morgue, with two motionless heaps in the middle.

Their large room was filled to bursting with a heap of unopened boxes, mostly containing radios or what was then called Hi-Fi.

Yousef was a quiet little man with a plastic-bald-scalp whose tiny uncle collected him for tea on Sunday.

Madan had a greying beard and a straying left hand.

He had a wife on Manningham who no-one ever saw.

I often saw him smiling sagely to himself or chuckling secretively into his shirt sleeve.

He had more wives and children than I've had hot dinners, as the saying goes.

One of his wives reputedly spoke in English.

Next door Peter occupied the chamber.

"Haven't you made my bed yet?" he demanded sternly in the corridor.

"You won't forget. Be sure to turn the sheets up properly won't you!?"

I never saw a single crease or crinkle in his bedclothes. I often wondered if he stood all night at the window peering up at the stars.

Most of his days were spent scurrying back and forth from the telephone or travelling on the double-decker to see his beloved daughter.

Peter said that he had once been a desk clerk at Brown and Muffs. That was shortly before the big fire, which gutted the place I understand...

He seemed intelligent enough but it was only when I saw him peeing at the bus-stop one day that I truly appreciated the extent of his handicap.

There was a strange odour lurking in the passageway between his quarters and Margaret's oak-panelled cage.

Some of my fellow work-colleagues referred to her as "the mucky old cow." Or, "that bitch who won't do as she is told."

I believe her incontinence was due to a *medical condition.*

It was a pleasant room filled with cuddly toys and an Everest of moth-eaten pillows. Pictures of her young relations. She'd never been married herself, although a rumour circulated that Sam had once asked her.

Margaret needed the stair-lift to get up to her room. She was getting on a bit...

I always found her bright and cheerful.

When we played our first game of 5's and 3's I could see that she had great difficulty holding all the dominoes.

I was told by Tracy that she was a "spastic!"

She had a smile which reminded me of my grandmother but she was a lot taller.

In a secluded corner of the establishment lived the behemoth Philip.

He'd been sent there as part of his court order, for molesting small boys.

'Curse of the home-helps!' it said in his file. He flew into fits of laughter about that.

Philip reminded me of Uncle Fester, only I think Uncle Fester had a lot more hair, with his toothless grandfather grin.

I don't know why they kept sending him to the barbers up the road because when he came back he never looked any different.

When I asked her who she liked best she said that it was 'Philip.'

She let him fondle her hand and make crude innuendos.

"Oh, he's harmless. Just a gentle giant," she said.

When I first arrived at Brookevale Philip was always going out to look at my car. He was always reporting its whereabouts.

After a while he was always asking why it was still there and when it was my time to leave.

Down the landing David shared with Keith.

David was a middle-aged Scotsman with grey short-cropped hair.

He'd lost his mother when he was five and had been badly crippled after a car hit him crossing a road not long after.

He was always friendly and eager to please but had a tendency to slip out to the shops in only his slippers.

I don't know why but he was always confusing me with the Manager, who was a lot younger than me and far better looking.

The police had once brought him back in a cop-car after he had been spotted fishing in the lake in only his underpants.

Keith was very close to his brother.

Keith's brother and his wife were regular visitors to the home.

Whereas Keith was tall and lean his brother's neck was a lot closer to the ground and he liked a good curry.

They brought his father's old railway books or pictures of the Dales.

The cellar store was filled to bursting with his father's old clothes.

Keith was about the same age as me yet he still suffered from teenage acne: or the 'dreaded lurgy' as we used to call it.

He's the only man I know who could take four hours to have a shave and still miss the long blonde hairs growing underneath his chin.

I once took him for a walk down to the shops just after his giro arrived and turned round to find him hoarding a stack of Fry's chocolate creams down his pants.

He hardly ever came down from his room. He seemed to prefer to talk in the middle of it.

When he did go into the lounge he was continually emerging from his chair and would hold his hand self-consciously up to his face to make any kind of conversation. At other times he remained in a state of *catatonic catalepsy.*

If I ever visited his room I found it hard to recognise him in the darkness.

His coal-like teeth gleamed at me from the edge of the mattress. Keith's railway books would be strewn on the bed along with a raunchy copy of Mayfair if he had been able to take one down from the shelf without shaking himself to pieces.

Keith moved like someone in a space-suit. He usually took long and forthright strides, lifting his foot with deliberate intent, but could hardly climb out of bed in a morning.

He once announced that he would not be going up to the corner shop again.

Some of the school pupils on the street had been giving him the third degree.

Nidderdale, Dentdale, Wensleydale. Can you think of another Keith?

Keith would reel them all off instantaneously.

His brother had once taken him on a camping holiday in the Dales many years before.

That was before Keith's infatuation with 'Catherine Slack' – a place rather than a person I'm assured.

At the top of the house lived our youngest resident.

He had once been in a rock band.

Paul attended a programme called the Cellar-project.

He was always waiting for his mum to collect him for the weekend.

I noticed the nervous way he laughed at inappropriate moments.

I seemed to happen if there were any people around.

Paul had suffered at least one major break-down that I am aware of.

He could be bright and sunny then as grim-as-an-undertaker.

Further down the corridor slept Roy.

A pleasant and amiable fellow with ashen hair and a haggard Dachshund smile.

I saw him frequently at the hall mirror examining face.

He often patrolled the home at night: another resident who was as restless as a jumping bean.

Then I wouldn't see him for days. I was dispatched to his room after four days of abstinence to see if he was still with us.

Doris said that you couldn't take a s...t without him telling the Owner what had happened.

Roy had once been a resident at Eastwood before it closed down.

He had a slight learning disability, became my *confidante* and guru.

He had once been a member of my walking group before the snitches got to work.

I found him genuine and down to earth. Much wiser than you would have imagined.

Next to him dwelt Christine: the 'fire-bug.'

She swears to this day that it wasn't her who burnt down the shopping-mall.

Before appearing in court she shaved off all her hair.

I do not believe this had anything to do with her religion.

From her early childhood Christine had been systematically abused, rejected and maltreated.

Her first act after welcoming me to the home was to buy me a brand new watch for Christmas. It was still only August.

She had retractable false teeth, ginger hair, soft hands, and a 44dd bust.

The cook asked her if she stored any treasure in it.

Christine was always throwing her arms around me and telling me how much she liked me.

I diplomatically turned down all her other offers.

She told me once that she was worried, because she had missed a period.

Her and Roy had been at it for months apparently.

Gordon warned me that she could be very manipulative.

Across the landing lay a double room where Rosemary rested her white head.

She was the same age as my mother but plumper.

Her cheeks were always flushed and she talked with her hands covering them.

She had a warm and glowing smile.

I often found Rosemary smiling at me across the room.

We went out for a walk one day: she got out of breath.

I helped her to walk up the hill to the bakers and back to the house again.

Rosemary just couldn't seem to hold down her food. After each meal I could hear her in the lavatory...

She liked a cuddle. Oh, so she *was* human...

Her two sons never visited. Her daughter had disowned her.

We had very few visitors in fact, except for nursing staff and *benefits*.

Paul's mother, or ex-residents wishing to refresh their memory, or those who found themselves in *emergency admission*.

I had whizzed in early that morning on my bicycle to find Rosemary collapsed in a ball on the hall floor just near the door to the dining room.

Her face had gone all purple. I never saw it again.

I often hear her voice though, as I do many of those residents from long ago, the former residents of Brookevale, who welcomed me with such undisguised warmth and affection on my arrival there in August 1996.

"You won't ever leave us will you Andy?" begged Christine.

David wanted me to take him for a ride in my new motor car one day.

Veronica shared with Rosemary…

I cannot tell you exactly when I first became aware of my feelings.

I had been there three or four weeks when I first became conscious of her footsteps as they trotted across the carpet to her chair...or the tremble of her hand, or the enduring fluctuations of her voice. When I walked in the room I tried desperately not to sit next to her but these damned feet just wouldn't listen.

I was spending far too much time in the TV lounge. I even watched Dale Winton's supermarket dash because of her. I bought some food for the cat. She scolded me for spending my money.

Philip reported me to her for stroking the cat while she was out of the room. It even had its own lap-cloth.

Veronica always looked after the cat. I was sternly rebuked for disturbing 'Smokey's sleep.' Even the rabbit was called 'Smokey.'

I suddenly found myself sitting on the stairs outside her room.

It was her first night alone in her new room and I could hear voices calling through the walls. Was Philip in there...?

I heard is voice, then I heard Veronica reply that she was alright in there by herself.

She stepped from the door into the small passageway to turn off the light.

She looked through the glass at me.

"Wish I was a cat!"

I don't think she heard me, but she might have done.

When I asked her about the past she told me to "mind my own business."

She did tell me shortly after that she had once worked in a wool-mill.

No matter how I tried to avert my eyes they always seemed to stray back to the source of my affection.

Except for the toothpaste I once borrowed, I never asked for any special favours, but made her meals, washed her dishes, ironed her sheets, and tidied up her bare and spartan room, tended to her every need, for three pounds an hour.

I'd have done it for nothing.

I was invited into the video lounge to watch *Pretty Woman*.

It was the first time I ever dared to sit next to her.

She had come to look at my album and offered me some fruit.

She told me she didn't like sweets.

"I haven't had many boyfriends," she suddenly stammered.

"'But you must have had plenty of interest," I said. She reminded me of a young man I used to know.

Veronica told me about a chap in her teens who kept asking her to go out with him.

He had even asked her mother why she wouldn't go out with him.

She said that he was the sort of man who always expected girls to say "Yes!"

That's why she said; "No!"

When she saw him months, or was it years later, as he walked down the pavement with his wife he had ignored her, even when she said "Hello..."

I reached into her bag of plums.

"You do have a lovely smile," I said. I can be a bit corny sometimes, but I meant everything I said. Had I said the right thing. Had I been too eager? Her glowing smile filled my heart.

"Besides your father and mother has anyone ever told you they loved you?"

She appeared wistful, or perhaps she just thought I was a nosy bugger.

I wondered how long it had been since anyone hugged her or put their arms around her.

She smiled. What could she have been thinking?

She told me that her brother had abandoned her and that she had only seen him once in two years.

He'd arrived at the home to take her to her mother's funeral and drive her back again.

Janet said that Veronica would come to you in her own good time.

As she sat down she flicked up her skirt. She stuck out her chest.

She had a lovely figure.

She murmured something about what people could get up to in their room. I must admit to questioning my hearing if not my sanity.

But those kind of thoughts were not in my mind.

The rules clearly stated: _'only females can accompany females to the park.'_

She looked at me intensely.

There were times when her deep brown eyes almost touched my skin. The pupils in her eyes grew into giant lagoons at midnight. They teemed with springwater.

When I told her how much I enjoyed her company she sounded shocked.

"And you were so kind to Rosemary."

I asked her what kind of clothes she liked a man to wear. She described the exact same clothes I had worn at my interview weeks before.

Christine blustered through the door with her blouse unbuttoned.

She tugged impatiently on my arm to play _bridge..._

I thought that I would rather watch _Robin and Marian._

Christine said that Veronica was still a virgin.

When she had first arrived Roy had asked her to go for a drink with him.

He told me that he didn't think Veronica wanted a relationship with anyone and that she was extremely shy.

"She's had boyfriends. Oh, Veronica was nearly married once!" he assured us.

Roy entered the room with a newspaper behind his back.

He peered unblinking across the lounge.

"Alright, Veronica?" he asked.

"I'm alright Roy," she replied.

I asked why such an apparently normal woman came to be living in such a place.

I was told that she had not been able to look after herself properly.

I walked into the lounge.

"Alright Veronica?" I asked.

She answered in the affirmative.

"Well, what are you doing in here then?"

And some of my jokes have been even worse than that...

But I did have to compete with Coronation Street.

Veronica hardly batted an eyelid if anyone came in.

She did remark that I was fit.

Her eyes lowered.

I can be such an idiot at times.

I went to read the so-called *expert's diagnosis* in the filing cabinets when no-one else was around.

With a label like that Veronica would have been lucky to find a job licking stamps.

I read the description written by a work-colleague of mine: 'Middle-aged woman with thinning brown hair and warts down the side of her face....'

I thought it was cruel.

Veronica had begun by suffering from a bout of depression.

I noticed that she had to have injections every few weeks.

While I had the keys I had a good look round.

It was wrong of me but I was very curious about her.

She had a lot of nice clothes but never went out.

Her only regular appointment was with *the chewing-gum lady* at the hairdressers up the road.

I think she also went to an art class at the hospital many miles away.

"Cilla Black's *never* had nice legs!" she suddenly demurred.

I just wanted to protect her.

But I still entered her secret garden and invaded her private space.

Many's the time I gazed at her old school photograph.

She complained that they had once put her in the running team.

I rooted through her decaying and dusty papers and fell into a bottomless well.

She was a Polish princess, locked in an ivory tower, more delicate than a lanterned flame.

More beautiful than any earthly flower.

Small pieces of broken china and a photograph of her late mother in the nursing home resting on the chest of drawers.

A discarded brassiere on the floor at the back of a lamp.

A lady's brown hair-piece discreetly hidden underneath a stock-pile of underwear.

The final receipts to the home she had lost. Her father's death certificate. It was quite a shock.

An old pair of black knickers in a wooden box for special occasions...along with a letter from her brother about his first born.

I left a very brief statement in an old purse at the back of the drawer, along with two ancient bus tickets. God knows when she would find it, if she ever did...

It was like trying to solve the mystery of the Sphinx.

I returned time and time again to disturb the contents of her drawer on each occasion moving the purse a little closer to the handle examining what I had written.

Until the day I returned to find a shawl draped over the edge.

 She wore her mother's silver wedding ring.

I had a daft idea about buying her a hat.

She had strong hands, quite large with long broad fingers.

I once read her fortune.

There were a myriad of lines in the centre of her palm.

She sat resolutely in her High-chair, her digits wafting beneath her nose.

She sighed and crossed her arms.

Her skin was pale and worn, but I could only see what she might have been.

I could only see a tenderness within.

I imagined that I could travel through time.

I was a scientist who after many years had tracked her down from another world.

With my knight's sword I would hack down all those years and push aside the stones, wipe away all those cruel cobwebs. I would restore her faith in men and with a single kiss would bring her back to life again.

She turned towards me and stared intensely into my eyes.

"I hardly came down from my room for ages," said Veronica.

I paused.

It was then that I realised I had seen her before when I was no more than fourteen, in a vision, long before I had even heard of Brookevale.

Veronica stood in the kitchen doorway.

"Someone's been sending me 'love-letters!'"

I almost fell through the floor boards.

"Don't tell anyone!"

Days later she hovered at my table.

"I didn't mean it," she said. "I do like you. Except when you tease me."

David asked her if she would fancy 'him.'

"No chance!" she laughed.

"What about Simon then?"

"No chance!" In equally derisory tones.

I asked her if she trusted me.

"I wouldn't say I did, and I wouldn't say I didn't."

Had the malicious tongues been wagging again...

I stamped out of the room.

When I returned a few days later everything seemed a little cooler, more distant, far more alone.

It took me three more days to pluck up courage to say anything to her.

I invited her to come and talk to me. She looked a bit worried.

"What about?" she asked me.

Yousef was in the video lounge rocking in his chair. He would be.

He stopped the minute we entered and sat down.

I had to make the best of it.

Where else could I go...

I began by saying how sorry I was.

Yes, I really did.

I think that I told her what a terrible wicked thing I had done.

I reached to hold her hand.

It made me very happy.

Her hand was soft, yet firm. She gripped hold of mine.

Just touching her was the most romantic thing I have ever done.

She glanced upwards when she thought I wasn't looking.

"I thought that you were teasing me again," she said.

As I leant forward her mouth tilted towards mine and her tongue mirrored my own, but instead I kissed her cheek. It is something I have regretted ever since.

I didn't want to take liberties and I thought it would be going too far.

"It *was me* who sent you those two notes" I said.

"I do love you very very much."

She began to tell me about a dream she had about me, but then she stopped.

"I find it very hard to put my feelings into words," she said. "You must be very brave!"

What else could I do?

I patted her on the back, got up and opened the door for her.

Yousef was grinning in his chair.

I thought about asking her to the pictures. She had gone with female members of staff...or feeding the birds in the pond, as she had done with Rosemary, but I shied away.

During the days and weeks that followed there was a thorn in my flesh which wouldn't heal. She thought that 'Platonic' meant 'not-serious.'

I held her hand only once more and left her in limbo.

I thought of the children she could have loved or of bending down on one knee and offering her the remote control to the enormous new television set.

I thought of inviting her to tea, with Christine?

Roy told me that Veronica could dance an Irish jig.

The Owner suddenly appeared a little more studious on his visits.

He ordered Roy to chop down the apple tree.

I should have had someone I could talk to.

Veronica's keyworker had packed it all in after all the bickering and mud-slinging.

The Owner said he could always replace a member of staff but a resident was another kettle-of-fish. They each brought in a tidy sum...

He warned me that the Residents were even worse than the staff for stabbing you in the back. I hoped he didn't mean it literally.

A work colleague said that I should never trust any middle-aged women working in care.

I was told by one middle-aged lady that men were a lot more honest.

A note appeared on the staff board.

It said that a wage packet had gone missing, and I heard the cook say something about missing food ending up in Firzhana's coat.

We were ordered not to speak to her or let her anywhere near the building.

Tracey told me that Veronica had gone to her with my notes. She smiled at me. I don't think she meant me any harm.

"We thought it was you!"

I blushed.

Gordon commented that he didn't think I would be there for very much longer.

"Please don't take this the wrong way...how can I put this" he always began...sucking his gums and clicking his tongue. Eventually I confided in Christine.

Her initial reaction was: "She must be very flattered. If you want my honest opinion Andy: it's unprofessional. You are one side of the fence. We're the rejects on the other side to you."

"You sound as if you are *lovesick!*"

"I only wish it was me."

"It's just an infatuation. Eventually you'll get over her and come to me. She'd be a stiff as a board and frightened to death of having sex."

"I love you to bits!"

"I didn't want to hurt you. Veronica said that she doesn't want a relationship with anyone and that she is quite happy on her own. She said that she is *too old.*"

"She said that it would have been different if she had been twenty years younger and *not living at Brookevale.*"

"She's happy as she is."

Even Roy offered his commiserations.

"You'll just have to cool it for a while. I always let them come to me. Keep doing your pumping iron Andy lad!"

"Talk to her. Just ask her for a quiet chat. I think she's bright inside. Intelligent..."

But the atmosphere seemed to suddenly change among the staff. For the first time I became conscious of some Arctic weather conditions.

Janet had asked me to go for a drink once. She suddenly became snappy and impatient.

Christine continued to throw her arms around me but surprised me by saying she was 'caught in the middle.'

The middle of what?

"Are you alright Andy? Do you fancy a cuppa?"

She fondled my hand religiously and offered to massage my head in the porch.

"How come you aren't married. You aren't gay are you? Tracy and Gordon both are."

"I love you Andy," drawled Christine. "You love me too don't you!"

Veronica smiled and nodded her approval.

She stood up as the cat meowed, its tail waving in the air...

"I do love her," she sighed.

I was so tense with her I could hardly utter a word.

Christine said that Veronica was very popular but she could also be very cruel.

She encouraged Veronica out on walks but she said that she was always looking round to see if there was anyone behind her.

"Eeh! She's lovely....Veronica!" smiled Roy across the dining room.

Her lips began to stretch exposing a small amount of gum.

A line of teeth appeared into a gentle and adorable expression.

Roy brought in her fruit, usually a banana, or a carton of yoghurt from the cellar.

I wouldn't watch her eat it though.

When Madan came back from town there lay the most enormous chocolate éclair in a bag.

I looked around and she had gobbled it down.

I imagined Veronica flying around the world in a wishing-chair, the Sun's rays lighting up the skies. That same look upon her face.

Time would stand still.

Below her would be all the poisons and trickery of this life.

The dark legs of her chair took on an animal form.

I hesitated, lest it rebuke me.

Where she flew nobody knew.

I was caught in a web of confusion. Her chair became like a holy relic.

Dare I approach? Would it suddenly take flight and zoom through the roof.

One day I found her sitting in the video room instead.

White skinned and sober.

To my surprise Madan was skulking round the corner.

On the coffee table before her lay a selection of cheap and tacky jewellery from *Bombay stores.*

The price tag was still on them.

She went to sit next to him and slithered alongside when I sat down.

"We were only watching a video," she hissed.

A day later I passed over her at the Resident's meeting.

That rather took the wind out of her sails, but I could see she was genuinely hurt.

She looked towards Christine.

"Are you sure?" I asked her.

"I've nothing at all to say," she answered.

Christine told me that Madan had asked Veronica to go upstairs with him, but she had refused.

"I'm not like that," she said to me.

"I'm so glad."

I began to knit my brows and sulk. She didn't know where she was with me.

She began pushing Philip away when he started mauling her hands which had to be a positive outcome though.

I came in one morning to find them both sat together in the porch.

Then in came Claudio.

"You are only being like this because I said he was good-looking!"

He'd only been there a week and already I was jealous. It couldn't go on.

I already had bags under my eyes.

"I still feel as if I'm only eighteen," Veronica said.

Claudio was only nineteen. A new starter.

A University student.

I started spreading it around that she fancied him.

"She's old enough to be his grandmother," sneered Christine.

 "She probably does," said Roy. "But we men have got to stick together anyway."

"Such a nice lad. Ever so nice. And I can't usually remember their names. If only I was a bit younger," smiled Veronica.

She whispered something to Janet, who began to snigger.

"I'll have to watch out for him then," she said.

I was fuming inside and sick to the core.

She returned to the dining room.

"I do not fancy Claudio at all," she said. "I do not have a crush on him and I am not after him at all."

I nodded at the screen where John Fashanu was compering the *Gladiators*.

"What do you think of him?" I asked.

"I like him!" she replied.

"Thought you would..." I said.

She reflected for a moment before rising from her chair and leaving the room.

She strode to the door. A ripple of emotion had momentarily run across her face.

I could see that I had made a big impression.

Madan told me that they were about to get married.

Christine would not tell me what they had been talking about but as I left she tried to force me to kiss her.

I suddenly received a phone call from my manager asking me to come in for an urgent discussion. And no it couldn't wait until I was next on duty.

"Is it serious?" I gulped.

He would not tell me anything over the phone but it set the alarm bells ringing.

I waltzed in through the entrance and stuck my head in the lounge.

Veronica froze in her seat. She was sitting alone again in her usual spot.

I said hello, and she responded.

Good morning?

She paled and hesitated to reply. She didn't turn a hair.

I was wearing a green hat from Granary Wharf. I was almost green myself.

A new member of staff frolicked with some Residents in the far corner. No-one batted an eyelid. The cook ignored me completely.

Diane was a white as a ghost.

I went downstairs into the Manager's office.

When he questioned me I began by denying that I had sent any love-letters. Just a few heartfelt words.

They were anonymous and had been thrown away yet were still presented before me as evidence of my illicit love.

Christine's writing was large and voluptuous.

Her words were honest and well-intentioned.

Veronica's writing was jumbled. There were large spaces between some of the letters. She had even miss-spelt her own name.

It looked as if she had been practising the spelling on a sheet.

Veronica had once told me that she had never managed to finish reading a single book and that it was her mother who taught her how to read:-

'Andy said that he loved me, and that he was always thinking about me....'

'The other one said that he didn't love me any more because of what I said.'

'He stroked my fingers.'

'He left an 'apple' under my pillow.'

'I didn't know what he was going to do next!'

"Well, what do you have to say about this Mr Hepworth?"

"You cannot go around declaring your undying love for a *Resident.*"

"If you had come to me before any of this got out we could have talked about your feelings."

"You've worked in a caring role before. You know about all the rules!"

"You must be either very naïve or very stupid. I cannot let you go on harassing one of my Residents. I had to practically drag this out of the staff. I am not going to treat you any different to anybody else. How could I ever trust you again after this?"

"None of the Residents would ever respect you again."

"They aren't monsters!" I said. "They are just human beings. It usually makes someone feel a lot better knowing someone cares about them."

I think I even said something like; "that which is done out of true love always takes place beyond good and evil."

My letters were gathered in evidence but my feelings were tossed in the gutter.

He handed me the blank sheet of paper which had been silently lingering.

"You can either resign or be sacked, it's up to you!"

"If Social Services got wind of this they would hold a formal enquiry and there would be all hell on. They might even get us shut down."

"They'd ban you from every home in the area. They'd paste your name on every outcast list they had."

I was even warned against 'Stalking.'

Then I was escorted to the door and refused permission to talk to anyone.

I tried to say goodbye but was ordered immediately off the premises.

He suggested I might write, but then he changed his mind and forbade me from making any sort of contact.

I suddenly fell into a pit of despair.

A world dressed in black surrounded my every move.

For weeks I suffered the most horrifying nightmares both night and day.

Dreams in which I was forever searching a maze of scattered rooms with a single word in my head.

One in which she fell headlong down a cliff on a walking group.

Roy stumbled after her.

I called her name distraughtly from the edge, but to no avail.

I just couldn't see her.

In one of my dreams I actually managed to get through.

She told me that I should not have treated her in that fashion when she was ill.

My sister put the phone down and didn't want to speak to me again about it.

She had been more interested in finding out which home I had been working in than my feelings.

She seemed to think that my *firing* had been nothing but a formality.

I'm sure she was right about that.

My mother, a retired schoolteacher, said that I should have waited at least a year before telling her about my feelings.

She accused me of manipulating poor Veronica's feelings and that I was being totally selfish.
She said that if I really cared for Veronica I would leave her in peace.
My stepfather said he thought there was nothing wrong with me having a relationship with her. Veronica was a grown woman of fifty, and I was ten years younger.
I was grateful for his support.
In desperation I thought of whisking her away to some deserted farmhouse out west where at least she could get to know me before my draught of hemlock, or my being put in irons, but it would have frightened her.
The former police sergeant I worked for part time offered to get her out of the building for me with the help of his assistant.
It did make me smile.
I needed to meet her in a place of gentle rapprochement on a sunny side of the street. I didn't want to be a thorn in her side.
My soul sat upon thorns.
For an instant I saw myself approach the park bench where she sat.
Then my aunty rang.
She told me that I would eventually get over it.
I had been seeing the doctor for *anxiety.*
My aunt still thinks I would have made someone a great husband and a loving father if I had only been given a chance.
I suppose she still remembers me as I used to be.
'How could you possibly love someone like that,' she gasped.
I wrote to the house but no-one replied.
Her brother handed my letter straight back to the management.
I phoned, but she was in the bath again.
The only thing which kept me going was the thought that I might see her once more.
I published my first anthology of poetry.
I sent her one red rose and a small gold cross on a necklace.
'Although this flower will fade my love for you will never die.'
I never saw the bouquet of flowers from Interflora on St Valentine's Day but I am reliably informed that they were delivered successfully with the following message inside:

'Je vois s'epanouir vos passions novices:
sombres ou lumineux, je vis vos jours perdus;
mon coeur multiplie jouit de tous vos vices!
Mon ame resplendit de toutes vos vertus!'

When the weather was fine I cycled up the hill past Harry Ramsdens. We used to go there when I was very little with my dad.
I couldn't find her brother's house at all. I suppose I just wanted to see if there was any family resemblance.
I eventually found the house she had shared with her father and mother.
It was on a small council estate. The local kids watched me with amusement.

I'd had a dream many years before about a woman screaming in a dried up river-bed. It had haunted me for years. Strange coincidences. I awoke in cold cold sweat. I couldn't see where the sound was coming from but my heart was beating like a drum.

Just months before my arrival at Brookevale I had been kissing a strange woman in a dream. She was kissing me with a warm and urgent passion.

Then a name had been whispered to me. I tried to scribble it down when I got up. It was so uncommon that I thought I could never forget it.

She had brown hair and her face was aglow. Her hair was combed down the side of her face like 'Veronica Lake.'

Her tip touched the corner of her mouth.

Veronica's former home was completely empty so I went next door to speak to the neighbours.

I knocked at the back door where I could see a woman of about the same age working in the kitchen.

"I'm trying to trace an old friend," I said.

"I'm afraid I haven't been round for a while. I wonder what could have become of her..."

Her husband suddenly appeared from nowhere....

"What was her name?" he asked.

She turned to him.

"Veronica, yes that's it Veronica."

He offered to give me directions to her brother.

"Do you happen to know what's happened to her?" I asked.

"Haven't you heard?" he said.

"She went mad! Veronica was taken away to High Royds nearly two years ago. She was having *screaming fits.*"

I started to shake my head.

What a miserable life.

"If you want my honest opinion," said the neighbour..."She was just lonely all by herself in the house: she hardly ever went out."

If only had been able to find her sooner perhaps she would never have got poorly because I wouldn't have let her!

I imagined us walking hand in hand somewhere peaceful.

Did she ever cry? I wonder.

Does she still sit in her High chair with its back to the window...

Does she even remember my name...

For years I sent her a card on her birthday and I always remembered to send her some roses.

'Binkie' the tabby cat stirred sleepily above the grate as she warmed herself in its rays on the ledge ...meow!

"There she is look!" exulted his mother alertly, pointing in an arc. A rustle. Legs of spindle-shanked tabby clawed in the shrubbery.

"She's making sure that you eat up all the rich brown eggs which she has made for you, or you'll never get hairs on your chest."

An old red hen pecking at some seed on the edge made his eyes open wide in wonder. Pearly whites and peggies. Playing the field, jumbo-sized.

"Where's Clara, where's Clara?" he murmured loudly. "There she is! I've seen her!" He dipped his husk in the yellow yoke. "Is this Clara's egg I'm eating Mammy? I'm not eating anyone else's you know!"

A musket shot! The haunch-tubbed Brobdingnagian thundered down the track...

Charging forth onto the spiney cartilage of the 'Snakeback' he could see some of the local kids speeding from their warrens on a lookout for Orlando's ice-cream van.

With a mien of certain fury he called his sister to sandblast or she would miss the amusing spectacle.

He squinnied at a familiar deity bumping towards them over the brow of the hill. The figure appeared from *Illium*, motioning mechanically over the hazardous scales as regular as clockwork.

He earnestly screamed for the others...
"Look Mammy. It's that funny man from up the road again," he laughed. He dashed into the middle of the twist so he couldn't be avoided by the stranger.

"Don't look at him," warned Mary. She even took in her washing. The bird teepeyed solemnly as he swore an oath over the ramp.

The '*Fantastic tumbledown man*' perambulated alongside the silvering pair perched astutely at the brink of their bay...everything was bigger in those days, even 'tumbledown' men! His sleeves did not match his hairy wrists, and the turn ups on his ashen suit exposed his rickety ankles...

17

"What was her name?" he asked.

She turned to him.

"Veronica, yes that's it Veronica."

He offered to give me directions to her brother.

"Do you happen to know what's happened to her?" I asked.

"Haven't you heard?" he said.

"She went mad! Veronica was taken away to High Royds nearly two years ago. She was having screaming fits."

I started to shake my head.

What a miserable life.

"If you want my honest opinion," said the neighbour..."She was just lonely all by herself in the house: she hardly ever went out."

If only had been able to find her sooner perhaps she would never have got poorly because I wouldn't have let her!

I imagined us walking hand in hand somewhere peaceful.

Did she ever cry? I wonder.

Does she still sit in her High chair with its back to the window...

Does she even remember my name...

For years I sent her a card on her birthday and I always remembered to send her some flowers.

Abdullah

New form of artificial intelligence

By <u>Lawrence van Der Splurgen</u> | Published: December 12, 2014 | <u>Edit</u>

For years Einstein laboured on his 'theory of everything' unable to discover a universal law.

Stephen Hawking has finally come up with the answer.

I can see him gleaming now.

Islamic flag found in nun's handbag

By <u>Peter Smith</u> | Published: March 25, 2015 | <u>Edit</u>

About one hundred anti-terrorist officers in the guise of football yobs raced across the capital today in order to lay their hands on a nun, who was carrying a banned motif in her handbag.

Along with the Islamic flag police discovered a large candle, some airline tickets, and a picture of the Pope.

Blame the devil

By <u>Peter Smith</u> | Published: March 25, 2015 | <u>Edit</u>

Members of the Evangelical church here in Aylsham are convinced that it is purely because we are tempted by the devil (or Satan as I affectionately like to call him) that we break the law.

Some of these people are allowed to vote and could actually be called up for jury-service.

It beggars belief.

The Cyclist

By <u>Adumla</u> | Published: March 16, 2015 | <u>Edit</u>

Many years ago I met a rather charming young Irishman who was a road-racing champion in his native country. He'd won all sorts of awards and was greatly admired by all who knew him. While working abroad he met a fifteen year old woman and began a relationship. She said she loved him. After being discovered he was sent to prison. From that moment his family totally disowned him. He was not allowed to contact any of them or to enter his home village and ended up on the street.

Bure Valley Sanatorium

By <u>Rumplestiltskin</u> | Published: March 12, 2015 | <u>Edit</u>

Spoke to Sonia over at the Rest home today. She was taking part in the bingo. Sonia has drooping tits and a four o'clock shadow. She's 27 stone, but used to be a marathon runner. For the last eight years she's been doing an OU course in Psychology and Social Sciences. Sonia said she was once six feet tall.   I guess she must have shrunk somewhat. Her family moved around a lot. Probably from tip to tip. She said she was related to *Queen Elizabeth I.*
"So were you married to Prince Charles as well?" I asked.

Comments

Jury members

By Peter Smith | Published: March 9, 2015 | Edit

The following Jury members will be sworn in at Bure Valley Sanatorium:

- *Crazy George*
- *Barry the Mute*
- *Harry the Gnome*
- *Barnacle Bill*
- *Blind Alice*
- *Keyhole Pete*
- *Double-chinned Mary*
- *Graham Stench*
- *Whispering Marian*
- *Poisonous Vera*
- *Gordon Seven Guts*
- *Pipe cleaner Ray*
- *Sister Thelma*
- *Doubtful Doris*
- *Olga the 'Ogress'*

Summary

In 2007 an obsolete firearm was found hidden away in pieces at my holiday home. I did not threaten anyone with it. I had simply been depressed and was thinking of a way to end my own life. I was being pursued by the police for contacting my ex partner. We had drifted apart because I didn't want her intimately. She had begun drinking heavily and was putting a lot of pressure on me to stay with her. I tried to look after her and her family and would not have hurt any of them in a million years. Close to the end of our relationship I admitted one offence of non-sexual exposure when a shop assistant saw me getting changed in changing room on a busy high street. She said that there was no sexual activity and that she had simply seen me naked from the waist down for 2-3 seconds. When the police arrested me two weeks later I was dragged through the town in handcuffs by four burly officers and held for ten hours in a police cell. Had I been a woman of a similar age I doubt if my life would have been turned upside down by such a minor incident. I understand that there were three or four squad cars in a race to get to my ex partner's house to tell her she was living with a Sex offender. Five years ago I tried to speak to her on the phone to explain my side of the story. It was neither malicious nor threatening. As a result of contacting her I was given two and half years in prison and had to serve the full two and a half years after being recalled for going on a library computer. This followed two years detention for the fire-arm offence and being on the run.

Near the end of my sentence a PPU Manager applied for a SOPO order in the Magistrates Court, claiming I was a dangerous Sex offender who would attack my ex partner or a member of the General public.

As a result of getting the order they were able to put me on the Sex offender's Register for life even though I had not been charged with any sexual offence.

Plebs: *I have a list of questions for you to mull over while you sift through some of my WEB-SITES:*

1 Wasn't it just a way to keep tabs on me because my sentence was over and you had no other excuse to harass me?

Have a look at the charge sheet. Do you see any charge of a sexual nature on there?

2 Why do you keep coming round to see me?

Why do you keep searching my home?

3 Why do you keep snooping through my private belongings and taking photographs of me and my home?

Would you like to snoop round my bedroom or pilfer through my wardrobe today? Would you like to examine my computer to see if I have watched any porn or tried to contact my ex partner? How would you like to have a good look through my private mail, or my private text messages?

4 Why are you always harassing me when I have done nothing wrong?

Why did you tell my mother that you 'only wanted to know if I was alright?'

5 Why do you keep banging on my door and calling through my letterbox when I'm asleep? Why did you threaten to break my door down if I didn't answer?

Why can't you ring me to let me know you are coming?

6 Why am I under MAPA when I did not commit a violent or sexual offence?

7 Why did you tell my neighbours and anyone who would come into contact with me that I was a dangerous Sex offender?

8 Why do you keep suddenly turning up at my door? What are you expecting to find.

9 Why do you keep treating me as if I am still in prison?

10 What do you think of officers who beat people up at the side of the road?

12 Why did you threaten to get a warrant if I didn't open my door?

13 What do you think of the fact that my ex had some of my property and lied about me selling it all at a car boot sale?

14 What would you say if I told you I was involved in a loving, caring, sexual relationship with a woman of my own age.

Why do you keep wanting to know if I have a partner or girlfriend?

15 Why did you follow me every day in your car (I recognised the number plate)?

16 Why did you contact the church and my Writer's forum to warn them I was a 'dangerous Sex offender,' and why did you turn up at their meeting?

17 Why do you keep wanting to know what I am doing?

RSVP BUNDERCHOOK

Sex mad Satan

By Peter Smith | Published: March 1, 2015 | Edit

Hi Simon!

As head of the local Evangelical church I thought you might like some feedback on some of my experiences with you.

1 We came along to talk to you about some bullying and threats we had been getting but you seemed far more interested in knowing whether we were having 'sex before marriage.' Why should an omnipotent deity who created all the known galaxies be remotely interested in our sex life? *I do apologise if our behaviour has undermined the reputation of the church in any way.* Why doesn't God simply destroy this Satan guy if he's causing so much trouble for everyone?

2 Did you hear Marshal in church this morning? I thought he was never going to shut up. An old man at the back of the church wouldn't stop laughing. They'll be taking him away soon.

3 I spoke to Peter about the monitoring of young people down at the Y.M.C.A. Do you really think this is the reason for him handing in his notice? As you will know, Pete is one of the church elders.

He looked at me as if I had a venereal infection when I told him I was in trouble.

4 Christine has been pressing me all day to talk to her about *wanking.* It is the source of great mystery to her. I cannot seem to get her to take any interest in politics or the world at large though.

5 Geraldine has lost a lot of weight but the pills seem to be doing her good. She was as 'high as a kite' when we spoke. She told me that she once had a wart on her finger and that after tapping it with the end of a bible it disappeared. I asked her if it worked on other body parts as well.

6 Joyce was very vocal once again. At one point I thought she was going to take off and fly straight to Paradise. It's a pity we don't really know what she's talking about, but I don't suppose that's any concern.

*May I wish all the self-righteous Tossers up at the church a very good day. Go in sin…I mean peace!

Comments

Irene

By Peter Smith | Published: February 25, 2015 | Edit

I've known Irene for a few years now. She's a sweet old dear with white hair and a daughter who comes in every Tuesday. Her daughter supports our morning coffee group, but is too afraid to tell her mum. Irene used to be the boss of a lady's Borstal down in London years ago. She's very shrewd and makes up her mind in an instant. Her daughter say's she's a bully. I quite like Irene though.

She sits quietly in her chair near the window while I offload all my anxieties and question her about the latest gossip here at **Bure Valley Concentration camp.**

Irene says she doesn't want to get involved.

Irene calls Christine 'Blondie.'

Irene can only identify people by their shape and tone of their voice now.

She told me they had been warned about me long before I came to live next door.

"The *man in the shorts*!"

So I thought I would warn *her cleaner* about the new warden about to arrive on the warpath.

A new rule had been posted and formal letters had all been sent out forbidding anyone from chaining their bike to the front rail.

"I've been doing that for years!" said Annette indignantly.

"It's really just to get at me," said I.

Irene said that she thought things couldn't get much worse.

I took Annette's bags down for her but passed Irene's door a short time later on the way back.

"Well, I don't want you talking to him," scoffed Irene. "I don't want him taking your bags down. Put them out last thing in future. I don't want anything to do with him!"

COMMENTS

Names that get you noticed

By [Godfrey Winklebacker](#) | Published: March 4, 2015 | [Edit](#)

Dear Mr Spigott,

I'm very surprised to hear that you have already fallen out with your *lead singer* and *drummer*. Your neighbours don't know what they're talking about. You were only trying to sort out their little disagreement.

I'm sorry my list of names has brought back unpleasant memories and that as a result of me attempting to think of a new name for the band it has caused you so much pain and anguish you have had to fall out with me again:

The Flying Pigotts Mucky pig/Dirty pig The Rebellion Fantastic Four The Maniacs Snot Wagon Under age Sex The Sleaze The Grunge The Piss-heads Phlegm The Daemons Fuck-neck Smeg-heads Pretty Spit

The stand-by

By [Rumplestiltskin](#) | Published: March 26, 2015 | [Edit](#)

My name is Tim Morgan and I'm a *standby*.   If anyone can't make it I'm your man. Sometimes when the leading man can't get enough lead in his pencil they call for me to lend a hand.

Ear growth

By [Peter Smith](#) | Published: February 25, 2015 | [Edit](#)

Researchers have discovered that the ear is the only human organ to keep growing throughout a lifetime.

First Contact

By Peter Smith | Published: January 26, 2015 | Edit

A PLACE TO TEST OUT NEW EXPERIMENTAL WRITING BEFORE IT GOES *LIVE. E.G.*

Dearest Mehmet,

I hope you don't mind me writing to you about the current situation. We were able to talk to Louise, which has helped us to reach a better understanding about what cunts you all really are. Having given your letter a lot of careful thought I have some further things I'd like to say:
1 I think in retrospect it was a bit silly of me to go exercising in the garden in full view of everyone. I can see it now as a mistake. I think it's possibly due to a difference in culture and outlook. It may even be a generational thing. I worked in the Health Service, so I am used to seeing naked bodies all over the place. I regularly attended a gym and swimming club, so seeing human bodies all around me was neither upsetting nor disgusting. I can see how it might be to someone with a different kind of upbringing or with a mental handicap. Even though there may be a bit of hypocrisy going on here I will endeavour never to behave so brazenly again. The last thing I want to do is upset anyone or make them feel uncomfortable.
2 I've always believed in human development and learning. I am quite a liberal minded person these days. Surely going to Court is both time consuming, distressing and expensive. Why can't we just hold out the olive branch to each other before, as in Louise's words "it has to go this far."
3 There has been no complaints of noise so far as I am aware concerning my own home, which is where me and Chris have spent most of our time during the last year in order to prevent any more complaints from her venomous next door neighbours. We have recently changed our routine to include a more normal sleeping pattern, which I think will have a better resolution for everyone concerned.
4 I do have a petition of about ten signatures so far from nearby Residents who are adamant we are considerate and responsible neighbours and did not act 'inappropriately' at the party. I have yet to get Fezile's signature about the left-over food which we had assembled for her because she was too ill to attend herself (having fallen at work): she is still away on holiday.
5 We totally refute any suggestion that there was anything unusual happening in the Reading room. We both know this is completely untrue. I would be prepared to stand up in front of anyone to deny this codswallop. I may have had my shirt off in there but that is because it is a nice quiet room where no-one hardly goes and I was doing my 'breathing exercises.' I am sure that a responsible caring Manager with your intelligence and foresight can see what is really going on here.

PS I went out for a drink with someone the other day. Why don't you let your friends at Big Brother know so they can send out a *general alert* and evacuate the town?

He came to sit and stare

By <u>Bird Dung</u> | Published: August 19, 2015 | <u>Edit</u>

I know this Baldridge.   We go back a long way.

When I first came out he crept from his dark fart stinking cess-pit and slithered along the path to sit and stare at me for two fuking hours. His putrid yellow eyes were eating into my brain. After that he brought along a whole host of his gang to sit and stare at me.

A life Baldridge. A life!

The back of my head feels like a cheese-grater

By <u>Adumla</u> | Published: August 2, 2015 | <u>Edit</u>

The back of my bonce feels all bumpy,

like a corrugated silver arc,

hard and obdurate,

to my fingers,

the puncture wounds,

of my youth.

Arian Grimblechuck: junior snoop-dog at the Norfolk surveillance academy and how we met

By <u>Sarin</u> | Published: June 12, 2015 | <u>Edit</u>

About six and a half years ago I contacted my ex partner to explain a misunderstanding and found her masturbating in front of her two young children to strangers on the Internet. As a result of ringing her phone number I received two and a half years in custody, and was forced to spend the entire sentence in detention. When I rang her number a policeman put on a funny voice and pretended to be her. Even the Judge said that he could not see anything threatening or malicious in the call. She also received one 'text' message from persons unknown.

Close to the end of my sentence DCI A man der Webbo applied for a special order claiming I was a serious danger to the public and that I would probably try to attack my ex partner on release. When I tried to say what a load of rubbish this was and I wouldn't hurt anyone in a million years I was told to be quiet. As a result of getting the order I was placed on a Register giving the police the right to harass and persecute me whenever they liked.

I first met Mr Grimblechuck, a short stocky man with slightly thinning hair and I presume a Sicilian ancestry, when he came to raid my caravan one morning. He demanded to know who I had been speaking to and threatened to have my door smashed in if I didn't let him in. You can see him in action on YOUTUBE: **Mafia hoods widen search for cami-knickers** (and others). You may know him. He likes chewing gum.

Mr Grimblechuck and numerous members of his gang continued to plague my neighbours with stories about me. I was followed wherever I went and in 2011 arrested after being accused of going on a Social Networking site. I was told that this would continue for the rest of my life. Six months ago my computer and recording device were seized on the pretext that I had used my step-father's surname when setting up an e-mail account three years ago, without informing them. On Wednesday I was eventually charged: with not telling the police about *all* my multiple characters.

I am 'legend,' I am many.

Best Wishes to *'Freckles'* by the way.

* Agent Grimblechuck has since been 'relocated' due to *staff shortages* and a lack of Spearmint at nearby knocking shops.

President Obama's daughter

By Godfrey Winklebacker | Published: May 28, 2015 | Edit

Barack Obama phoned me on the sky-phone the other night. He offered me the following in return for invading Iraq AND MARRYING HIS DAUGHTER:

truck load of ass-wipes

sixty cans of coke

five battle cruiser type two destroyers

seventy tanks

One health care voucher

A 1950's Hawaiian passport

Three law degrees from Harvard

An old birth certificate

An Indian Motel Reservation

Three Kentucky fried chickens

I said, "Mr President, there is no way I'm going to invade Iraq for less than seventy camels."

Comments

Nasty little Joan

By <u>Adumla</u> | Published: May 22, 2015 | <u>Edit</u>

I saw Joan down at the Friendship Hall today. She's a practising Christian like many more I could name. A Catholic in fact. Joan has suspicious eyes.

I was looking at joining a chess club or a History group when she entered the building.

"You see him over there don't you!" She bent down over a table of old-age pensioners.

"He was thrown out of Bure Valley. Don't talk to him!"

They all looked at me with horror.

I stood up and walked over to the table.

"Get your facts straight! I left *Bure Valley Zoo* of my own accord."

"And you are a <u>nasty old woman</u>."

POLICEMAN GUILTY OF FLASHING HIS TRUNCHEON

By <u>Adumla</u> | Published: May 10, 2015 | <u>Edit</u>

We had to pass by the home of a young constable on our way to school many years ago. We lads nearly pissd ourselves. I think we needed a positive 'role' model at that age. Mr Trundall would be standing outside his cottage waiting for the girls to come. He always smiled and said "hello boys!" but he seemed more interested in what was coming up the lane.

When we sat down in class the girls were always wild with excitement.

"Mr Trundalls been flashing his big hairy cock at us again Miss!"

We were slightly envious of him, but we waited for nature to take its course. Rumour was that he could actually slam his gate shut with it.

(Mrs Trundall would always shake her head. "Just wait till I get home!")

She was a great Headmistress.

I had to wait years before she could give me a good enough blow job though.

Not there yet

By <u>Adumla</u> | Published: April 23, 2015 | <u>Edit</u>

Dear Geraldine,

Thank you for the book about *Close to death* experiences. Time is very precious to me so I only scanned through it.

1 Your quote from Einstein summed it up really (believing in what is real, and not what you *want* to be there!). He was an atheist I think.

2 I presume the author comes from the American bible thumping belt and is hoping to promote his church. Is 'Eternia' a non-profit making spin-off?

3 You started out with a belief in heaven and you were already familiar with near death experiences. The dreams you read about simply confirm your beliefs. That's all they are: lucid dreams. But then dreams can take us anywhere. The human mind is a powerful tool and is part of the collective unconscious.

4 The writer wanted to believe in a place called 'heaven' but did not *prove* it existed, and did not prove the existence of 'God the Creator' either. Although, I have to say, it's a very attractive idea if you want a father figure.

5 This is all about *fear of death and oblivion.* The desire to believe we carry on in an idyllic place full of peace and tranquillity. Full of white lights gold carpets and angels.

Acts of the imagination when someone is physically ill and traumatised do not prove the existence of heaven but they do tell us that the human mind is very creative and alive. While we are in the state of dreaming we can receive information and impressions from the higher powers. It's open to interpretation who or what they are and where they come from.

Why would anyone want to return to this miserable world after being in such a place? It doesn't make sense. Unless of course, it were to return here to evangelise and make conversions. Why should darkness always be associated with evil and light with good? Why is *going up* always associated with 'God, or heaven?' It all seems very simplistic. Wouldn't it be boring though, to spend eternity just worshipping a bright light, unless you had no idea about the passing of time.

There is no place we cannot enter through our dreams.

* Incidentally, it is highly presumptuous to assume I will cease to exist when my physical body decays. My life and all the things in it will echo for an eternity, *free* from judgement or punishment. Christians used to scare people with the idea of hell, but now you simply say: "you will be lost to God forever!"

You say you have been talking to 'Jesus' since you were sixteen. I don't know who you have been talking to, but Jesus died about two thousand years ago. He turned his back on the material world. According to your organisation it's wrong to communicate with *dead spirits...*

Thank you for the weekly mass which is being said on my behalf and for your constant prayers; of course I will come to know the lord one day. I'm sure it will help to get me back on the straight and narrow…;-)

Not while Kevin's here

By Rumplestiltskin | Published: April 5, 2015 | Edit

I have a step-brother now, whose name is Kevin. He makes iron gates for a living. I am reliably informed that he is "normal!" His children came to live with him after his wife broke two of his fingers. I caught him on a dating site one day:
"Never paid for it in my life!" he said.

My mum bundled me towards the door.
"You'll have to go now. Kevin's coming."
She pushed me over the threshold and out into the garden.
"You know you can't come round if Kevin's here. You know what he thinks about people like you!"

I heard the bolt go on.

Total bollocks

By <u>Adumla</u> | Published: April 18, 2015 | <u>Edit</u>

Dear Judge Gilbertson,

I would like to give you some feedback on a case you heard recently involving myself. I know these cases are notoriously hard to weigh up but it seems as if you have gone along with all the stereo-typing presented to you by Wherry Housing. By granting the Injunction you appear to be accepting all the lies told about me.

My partner is not as vulnerable and helpless as Wherry Housing would have you believe. However, she was harassed by some of the women at the scheme long before I arrived. Only last year Wherry Housing investigated complaints about obscene notes being pushed through her letter box and her door being taped up. There is no mention of the swearing, abuse, name calling and slander perpetrated by her neighbour Christine D. (whose son is a serving police officer) over the last four years. I am not responsible for giving Mrs Didwell a heart attack or for the bruise on her arm which she said happened when I knocked her down on my bike (in the original story she said the bike had been left against a wall and it had fallen on her). She asks: "Why are they doing this to us?" She must be having a laugh. If the accusations against me were so serious (such as having sex in the garden in front of her grandchildren and running her down on my bike) then why didn't she go to the police?

Why have I been ordered to lock my bike in the bike shed when I no longer live at Bure Valley House and no longer have a key? Are you seriously saying I will be hauled in front of a Magistrate for putting my bike up against the wall of my partner's home?

What is to stop these malicious and vindictive neighbours from making up further complaints just to get us into trouble? *Christine D. and her friends said over two years ago that they intended to get rid of me and you have helped them to do it.* She actually made a physical threat against me and my partner in the hallway just after her accomplice told us to "Fuck off!" which was witnessed by a Support Manager some eighteen months ago (that's not the same Support manager who warned my partner to break up with me or face losing her bungalow). There was also a live bullet which was found planted in the laundry. It is total bollocks that we were "eating each other's faces off" at the Christmas party. The fire alarm is a safety feature and we turned it off at the first opportunity. It is us who live in fear of our lives. Miss Temple actually went to another neighbour's house with a knife in her hand to collect her lottery money. I didn't even know who David Low was until I read his statement. I'd never even spoken to him, although I do know he makes regular reports to the 'Committee,' and is a bald little prick!
Incidentally, a member of the Care staff has been parking her bike against the rails for years but has not been singled out or threatened with court action like I have. I can only assume this has all been about labels again. I do of course agree to abide by the instructions not to cycle anywhere in the area highlighted.

I am appalled that a District Judge of your standing should have taken any notice of the allegations that we were seen bonking each other in the Reading room. There were other allegations, for instance, that I streaked down the corridor without any clothes on. Do you really think we are that mad? Although the police were called by one of the gang after someone saw me sunbathing in the garden (I had been given permission to do so by the Project Manager Alex B).

Janine S. (obese ogre-woman with beard and drooping tits) states that she never actually saw me banging on her door or wall but that "It couldn't be anyone else." Mr Yahman (Wherry Housing) told me that they did not need to prove anything to believe it happened and so I assume you are siding with him. I did knock on her door but just to invite her to our social morning and when she didn't answer I walked away. I didn't know that was a felony in our country. I thought I was helping Miss Saunders by encouraging her to take part in our group. I know that she has had extensive treatment for many years. She often talked to me in an open and friendly manner when she was there about her relationship with the late Queen Mother. I am shocked that she should have been so easily manipulated into making these statements against me.

I did not try anyone's door or look through anyone's letterbox. I did not try to get in Miss Saunders flat while she was having a bath. Neither did I attempt to 'impersonate' a member of the Wherry organisation by offering to carry in someone's luggage. When I did try to speak to Mr Yahman (Specialist Manager/Circle Housing) he refused to speak to me. Is it my fault that half the Residents have bats in the belfry. Why do you accuse me of 'impersonating' a member of Wherry Staff, when all I did was offer to do odd jobs for someone?

 It is just not good enough to let these allegations lie. I'm afraid I will just have to try and get to into Court despite my poor third leg so I can cross-examine these liars about the nonsense they have told.

Thank you for waving the costs unless further trouble arises. My partner is even afraid to speak in her own living room in case she gets reported again.   Bure Valley Zoo has an awful reputation in the town which I didn't know about before I came to live there. We are extremely worried that it's only a matter of time before these malicious people make further complaints just to get us before you again.

Mrs D asked what I was doing at Bure Valley House because there didn't appear to be anything wrong with me.

Jesus as sex symbol

By Sarin | Published: March 24, 2015 | Edit
Geraldine stood up in church on Sunday with her right hand raised above her. The phrase: "tortured and stripped naked," tremored from her throat as her eyes flickered in rapture.

Mum's the word

By Rumplestiltskin | Published: March 23, 2015 | Edit

I hate asking for favours, but sometimes you just have to swallow your pride. I recently asked my mum for a small loan.

"Look mum. This is very kind of you, but I don't want to leave you short."

"You won't be leaving me short," she said.

"Yes, I will. You are only five foot."

(She still thinks Charles should be king).

Comments

0 comments

Circle Housing Spying and co-ordination Centre

By [Rumplestiltskin](#) | Published: March 23, 2015 | [Edit](#)

DEAR MR BUNDERCHOOK,

It has been brought to my attention that you are regularly parking your bike near to the main entrance of the scheme which goes against my previous requests for you not to do so. I must remind you that this is a Fire exit route and that there is a possibility your bike will prevent the very odd people living there from using the hand rails close by. It was reported that your bike interfered with the main entrance door over the weekend and that Fat-arse was unable to get her bum inside the building. It is perfectly alright for *Annette* to chain her bike to the rail though. She has been leaving it there for years. The paperwork for your Court injunction has been passed to our legal team.

Sincerely,
Senior Housing Officer

No need for cameras

By [Peter Smith](#) | Published: March 21, 2015 | [Edit](#)

The Specialist Circle law enforcement officers at HMP Bure Valley House have informed us that we do not need any surveillance cameras around the building. They would cost a lot of money and would need to be monitored (along with all the Residents) 24/7. I can only assume that we have them here already.

Comments

Computer programmer bags eight for grains of rice

By [Rumplestiltskin](#) | Published: September 19, 2015 | [Edit](#)

A computer programmer was given a sentence of eight years at the Crown Court today. The police spokesman could hardly conceal his glee.

The young man (who happened to be Asian) was simply trying to buy rice over the Internet, but was persuaded to take it in powder form by an FBI agent, posing as an agricultural engineer.

Comments

Lying MP's and Select Committees

By Usuli Twelves | Published: September 17, 2015 | Edit

We all heard the tape of Straw and Rifkind offering to ask questions for money.
These people certainly look after their own.

Nosey Parker head of M15

By Usuli Twelves | Published: September 17, 2015 | Edit

Yet more laws to monitor us all are finally on the way. The Government was bound to become fixated with this idea; they have found a way to by-pass reservations from the General public.
"We need to up-date surveillance legislation for the safety of you all."
Let's just hand over our house door keys to the police then!

Baldridge harassment of pensioners

By Peter Smith | Published: September 16, 2015 | Edit

We had a visit from the Plebs on Tuesday. They sneaked in through the back gate again. Baldridge used the excuse that I might have done a search for my ex-partner to root through my home, play space-invaders on my computer, and search underneath the bed. I asked them to leave several times but one of them kept asking the old lady if it was alright to stay. She was very confused. It's part of her illness.
I still don't know the name of his Moll, but I suspect he is giving her one on the side. He looks the sort of specimen who would take advantage of the young recruits. Although not as young as he would like.
We had to check the petty cash and fumigate the whole place after they'd gone.

Some day an extremely large eagle is going to defecate from a great height and will wipe that smile right of his face.

Anders Breivik where are you now?

By Bird Dung | Published: September 3, 2015 | Edit

Labelled as a psychotic killer for gunning down Christian Socialists out lighting fires he will probably spend twenty years behind bars. After that he could stand for Parliament.

George Osborne (Conservative Chancellor) blamed the current migrant crisis on:

1 ISIS

2 People traffickers

I rest my case your Honour!

Europe must do more says Merkel

By Bird Dung | Published: September 9, 2015

Doctor murders Muslims

By Usuli Twelves | Published: September 7, 2015

Doctor David Cameron proudly announced the death of several Muslim fighters today. These British Citizens were spotted on the ground by RAF Drones after conversations were overheard via the Internet. Talk about the cock which crowed before dawn.

He described their deaths as: *"entirely lawful!"*

AND,

"Our inherent right to self-defence."

"There was no other way! (to get your own back I presume)."

Well, if the *Attorney General* said it was right, then it must be…

In the name of the Egyptian people

By Usuli Twelves | Published: September 1, 2015 | Edit

As the three Journalists were sent to prison the Judge barked down at them: "In the name of the Egyptian people! I sentence you to three years for spreading false news!"

I wonder how many Western Journalists would escape a custodial sentence, or come to that anyone working for the Authorities?

Indian Villagers in favour of rape

By Usuli Twelves | Published: September 1, 2015 | Edit

An all male council of villagers has sentenced two sisters to rape for their brother's misdemeanour (one of them an old woman of fifteen). No wonder the Indian population is still on the rise. I hope the elders enjoy their *Sunday afternoons*.

On the same subject. The charges of rape against Julian Assange are to be dropped because the Prosecutors have 'run out of time.'

A curious phrase.

I wonder if the *British Police* will file a complaint?

Ten months for murder

By Rumplestiltskin | Published: October 21, 2014 | Edit

At long last Oscar Pistorius has been sentenced. I don't think we will ever know the truth about his motives and what went on that night, unless he decides to tell us one day.

The comments I heard were:

"Fair and just to society!"

"Justice has been served."

How can so called intelligent people make comments like this without falling about laughing?

I now understand that his defence team is going to lodge an appeal against the harshness of the sentence.

What must other men in prison be thinking?

You can get more than ten months just for looking at the wrong photographs on-line or for not telling the Authorities where you are living.

And those people have to serve their *whole sentence* behind bars.

Back in Iraq

By Sarin | Published: November 6, 2014 | Edit

The British and American forces are slowly creeping back into the country they were so quick to leave only a short while ago. Will someone tell me what the fk is going on??
I clearly remember Obama say he was going to withdraw his troops as soon as he possibly could.
A British General said that it was really just about "containment."

Came from a good home

By Rumplestiltskin | Published: November 3, 2014 | Edit

A sad mixed up little schoolboy who stabbed his teacher to death has just received twenty years. ~That's 'British' justice for you! I call on you to make sense of any of it.

Angels aren't real

By Usuli Twelves | Published: November 2, 2014 | Edit

If living a 'perfect' life and never doing anything 'wrong' makes you an 'angel,' then angels really are idealistic nonsense. If you said there were forces beyond our control and understanding then I would agree.

Kicking through Autumn leaves

By Sarin | Published: October 30, 2014 | Edit

Most of life is mundane and drab. There's that rare moment sometimes when all seems well. Like kicking through Autumn leaves on a sunny morning or finding someone you can love.

Grooming report

By Surloin Steak | Published: October 30, 2014 | Edit

They aren't children, they are young women, and it isn't 'rape!'

Comments

Marsham rave

By Surloin Steak | Published: October 30, 2014 | Edit

It's the policy of Norfolk police to come down hard on anyone organising or joining in with a rave (it's a sort of music festival without all the hype).

These are some of their comments after an 'illegal' rave was held in a deserted field nearby this weekend:

- "Extensive damage was caused to flora and fauna."
- "We had to issue 150 fixed penalty fines to motorists and campers."
- "Distress was caused to animals."
- "These were selfish individuals!"
- "We did it to maintain safety and limit harm."
- "We have seized all their music equipment to prevent it ever happening again."
- "It is upsetting and disappointing."
- "We are continuing our investigations."
- "These people think it's okay to trespass…"

Hog roast anyone?

Four legs good. Two legs bad!

Man tries to wipe Prime Minister's backside

By Rumplestiltskin | Published: October 27, 2014 | Edit

A young traveller named Dean Balboa Farley was arrested today as he jogged along a Leeds City pavement. His crime: getting too close to the Prime Minister. Mr Cameron's new hair-do was nearly spoilt during the escapade. The young male, with blue ear-wax dripping from his ear, complained he was assaulted by a proud British Bobby before he could explain his true motives.

He admitted that his body had accidentally brushed against the Prime Minister's tailored suit before he could even get his message across:

1. Less State intrusion
2. A more listening Government
3. The removal of old bull

* The Facebook page on which he *outed* himself has been instantly taken down.

New security measures were due to be announced by the Met very soon.

Government policy: the re-emergence of Nick Clegg the Liberal

By Surloin Steak | Published: October 30, 2014 | Edit

Who shall we pick on today?

I know. Let's pick on poor people. Anyone who can't get a Solicitor.

We'll stick our heads in the sand.

You know it's morally wrong to take drugs.   Let's give them **all** a criminal record.

(I don't take drugs. Alcohol and cigarettes don't count!).

Drug taking is part of the culture. **You don't have to take them if you don't want to.**

Comments

Derogatory remarks to footballers

By Lawrence van Der Splurgen | Published: October 29, 2014 | Edit

I am petitioning the Morpork Parliament to have a new law passed which will mean the flogging to death of any person making derogatory remarks about aging footballers, well past their prime.

The offence will include any remark posted on a social networking site (we won't be able to *prove* who posted it, but cameras in your living rooms is only a small step away).

The Samaritans

By Lawrence van Der Splurgen | Published: October 29, 2014 | Edit

The Samaritans are to join the Authorities in helping to spy on people and monitor any subversive thoughts. Their new 'radar' system goes into operation today.

* As Nietzsche once said: 'the thought of suicide is a powerful solace, by means of it one gets through many a hard night.'

There was a time when anyone who committed suicide would be buried outside the church walls. Anyone attempting suicide could be charged with a criminal offence.

£25 free Ebola kit

By Lawrence van Der Splurgen | Published: October 29, 2014 | Edit

Families in Africa will be offered a free Ebola kit to help them with hygiene and personal care. Cheap at any price.

Wear the T-shirt or else!

By Lawrence van Der Splurgen | Published: October 29, 2014 | Edit

Citizens of Great Britain will now be forced to wear T-shirts to make sure they espouse the correct political viewpoint. Some of them will say:

- **Dangerous twats**
- **We'll have you down the station**

The Royal Mounties

By Usuli Twelves | Published: October 24, 2014 | Edit

Appalling scenes greeted the Canadian public as a madman went on the loose in the Canadian Parliament. Fortunately, he was shot dead before he could do any serious harm. The *gunman* was cheered by the packed hall and clapped on his back as a hero. I saw him stand stony faced, not even a tremble in his hands.

"People of all faiths have expressed unity."

"The atmosphere was heavy with a sense of sorrow."

A soldier was shot outside the monument:

"I cry for the victim, but *not* for my son!"

"An outrage, on their own doorstep."

"Canada will not be intimidated by these non-Canadians! We will continue to be strong and open."

"We're the good guys!"

A Muslim inhabitant of the city said:

"I love these Canadians. They are so forgiving and friendly."

United States forces continue to pound Isis insurgents.

553 people have been killed in Syria since September…

Sir Cliff

By Lawrence van Der Splurgen | Published: October 25, 2014 | Edit

Apparently the raid on Sir Cliff Richard's home has caused 'irreparable damage' to his reputation and standing. Join the club mate!

Police harassment in the UK is on the increase and who do we have to blame?

Congratulations, and celebrations, when I tell everyone that you're in love with me!

Crone's disease

By Lawrence van Der Splurgen | Published: October 25, 2014 | Edit

I'm sick of hearing about new cures for cancer, hearts that beat on long after they should be still, and vaccines which deliberately keep people alive.

How about a little soap and water? Why should the *West* spend billions of pounds on research?

What is wrong with a little self control?

Twelve year old fathers

By Surloin Steak | Published: October 24, 2014 | Edit

When I was growing up in the nineteen-sixties several of my class-mates were already fathers by the age of twelve. I remember them helping to wheel the pram down to the nursery, with their satchels slung over their shoulders, still in short pants, and wearing their school uniforms. Nobody arrested them.

COMMENTS

Cost to the taxpayer

By Lawrence van Der Splurgen | Published: October 22, 2014 | Edit

New figures released today show that it costs the UK taxpayer £70,000 to deport each criminal from the country. Where's the money going?

I would imagine a lot of it goes on red-tape and Civil Servants.
For less than a box of matches I could accomplish the same result.
My wheelbarrow only needs a small drop of oil and we regularly hold bonfires at the end of the garden.

Dominic Cumberbatch

By **Surloin Steak** | Published: October 21, 2014 | Edit

Educated at Harrow. A rose from an acting family. Connected to Queen Victoria. Ancestors decorated. Drama teacher said he was the best schoolboy actor he'd ever *come across*. Took on the mantle of toad, or toady.

Tory bullshit

By Surloin Steak | Published: October 21, 2014 | Edit
I hear the Home Secretary is going to round up anyone who has been **radicalized** into voting UKIP>!

Snoopers

By Lawrence van Der Splurgen | Published: October 19, 2014 | Edit

My Gran was telling me about how tough it was in the nineteen thirties. A lot of people were out of work. She was doing her best to replace those sons who had fallen in the Great War. Wars are wrong our course, but it would soon be time for another one.

During the depression some families received as much as £1 per week to live on. If you were on the 'dole' one of the Government's 'Snoopers' could enter your home whenever they liked.

She was given a pot of jam as a gift one Christmas. No sooner had she opened the jar then two of the 'Snoopers' burst through the front door and raced into the living room. They demanded to know how much the jam had cost so they could deduct the amount from her benefits.

The last vanity of Joan Rivers

By Lawrence van Der Splurgen | Published: October 19, 2014 | Edit

What was left of Joan Rivers has finally returned to the soil.
I saw her once on British Television, where she had been given her own show. Without anyone to bitch at she was bloody awful.

So much for confidentiality

By Sarin | Published: October 18, 2014 | Edit

I had a letter from my doctor this morning reassuring me that the Authorities were never given information about patients without a written request. I know this to be a blatant falsehood.

There's no such thing as confidentiality.

Anywhere.

Library Surveillance

By Sarin | Published: October 18, 2014 | Edit

It's a fact that we are all monitored by Big Brother through the use of our library cards. Gone are the days when you could just waltz through the library door and ask to log on at the nearest internet connection. Cards are only issued when all your details have been checked. What can we do to protest? Governments, once elected, never listen.

I might add, that I am not recommending sabotage, even with a can of *Coca-Cola*.

State censorship

By Rumplestiltskin | Published: October 18, 2014 | Edit

What do you think about the demonization of Isis?

When do we ever hear the rebels speak for themselves other than through selective news reporting?

Why can't we be allowed to make up our own minds without being brainwashed by the Government?

Another mass killing in the US

By Surloin Steak | Published: October 17, 2014 | Edit

Its Autumn already and there's not been a decent High School carnage for weeks. I'm beginning to think the kids have run out of fire-power.

I suppose that's what happens when you keep picking on someone.

At my school Mark **Lynch** was the one to be singled out for ridicule. It was his misfortune to have ginger hair, and no amount of drinking slops from paint cans was going to put a stop to it. Each dinnertime he was pushed down the hill next to the running track by a gang of noisy yobs. That was until his mother took him away from school. To be frank, even if Lynch had access to a fire-arm's cabinet I doubt if he would have rid us of all the staff. He just didn't have the balls.

Ling however was another kettle of fish. He was short and swarthy. A sort of cross between Charles Manson and a miniature Rottweiler.

I've yet to hear of anyone going mad in the House of Commons or the Senate unless you count the invasion of Iraq. If anyone did manage to sneak something past the guards they would be spoilt for choice.

A bit like shooting rats in a rain barrel.

Government clampdown on free speech

By Surloin Steak | Published: October 17, 2014 | Edit

How long before the British Government, along with their Soviet counterparts, make it illegal to record the authorities bullying and intimidating everyone?
Why did it take until the long drawn out soap opera of 'Pleb-gate' before this Home Secretary was willing to admit that the British police are capable of lying, when it's a known fact that they have been telling porkies since the first truncheon was ever lifted in blue faced fury?

What is truth?

By Lawrence van Der Splurgen | Published: October 16, 2014 | Edit

When a writer like John Grisham makes a stand in defence of men you know it's all gone too far. No wonder the figures for rape have gone up when to be charged with rape *these days* you only have to look in the wrong direction. I can respect anyone who tells the truth. I can sympathise with someone who has been honest about why they acted like they did. But what happens when you speak out in defence of the truth.
As they used to say in Northern Africa: 'tell the truth and get your head knocked off!"
Why is it men always get the blame?

JESUS CHRIST

By Usuli Twelves | Published: October 15, 2014 | Edit

Just an ordinary man, in that he was trying to make some sense of life.
A philosopher, intelligent, sensitive, but still a rabbi.
Jesus Christ!

Farage By Usuli Twelves | Published: October 15, 2014 | Edit

Nigel Farage was recently asked if he intended to make any kind of alliance with the Conservatives.
'Why don't you discuss your concerns with David Cameron?'
"Because I don't believe a single word that David Cameron says!" stated Mr Farage, quite categorically.
Oh come on, Nigel!
He is the country's Prime Minister, after all…

Comments

Police State

By Usuli Twelves | Published: October 15, 2014 | Edit

ANOTHER NEW LAW
From today the punishment for sending a photograph of yourself to someone you like will have a two year jail term. I've heard they are about to make adultery unlawful too. Let's build a lot more prisons then. Plenty of them! **Comments**

Not enough snitches

By Usuli Twelves | Published: October 15, 2014 | Edit

We really don't have enough tell-tales in our society. What we really need are more people willing to go to any lengths to defeat a rival even if it means spreading a few false rumours. This is particularly true in the higher echelons of society where there is nothing more amusing than seeing a member of the Establishment brought down a peg or two.

Comments

Environmental Health

By Usuli Twelves | Published: October 15, 2014 | Edit

Traits such as dishonesty, aggression, and avarice have long been seen as negative by the 'moral majority,' yet placed in the right environment those same traits will ensure survival and success. This is extremely good news for those in power and for those preaching to the unconverted.

Humans with bigger brains

By Rumplestiltskin | Published: October 13, 2014 | Edit

Ordinarily I would say: *quality counts*. But it's an established fact that **size** does matter. When it comes to brain size volume does count. There is a direct ratio between intelligence and brain size. When apes first moved out of Africa their intelligence is reckoned to be about the same as the average 2-3 year old. Brains grew quickly as a result of having to lie, of having to outwit your opponent. Apes with larger brains were at an advantage.
In modern times the same thing applies.
It's really a question of 'mental fields.' Some minds are able to reach far beyond their immediate environment and travel to other plains.
They can read the thoughts of others, and even see into the future.

A fairer society (you're having a laugh)

By Surloin Steak | Published: October 13, 2014 | Edit

Today Oscar Pistorius will be sentenced for shooting his girlfriend through the bathroom door.

A Representative for the Correctional Services has suggested 'community service' as a suitable punishment, to act as a ***deterrent.***

If accepted Oscar will spend some of his time loitering with a broom handle, until that gets too heavy for him. Poor Oscar!

'Retching' at the prospect of having to spend a couple of hours alone sweet talking a sympathetic counsellor.

"He has lost everything: his youth, his prestige, his mansion, his wealth."   I can't imagine him making a single penny from any future book contract…and he will be forced to live in his Uncle's expensive penthouse. Poor him!

People who talk about a 'fairer society' have to be living in Noddy-land?

Greed

By Surloin Steak | Published: October 13, 2014 | Edit

A ravenous appetite for money and power still motivates the human population. I passed some health workers singing and supping cups of tea at their picket line today. When you think about how poor everyone used to be! MP's are about to receive their midterm bonus.

Cars pumping their fumes everywhere. A TV in every room, with no-one watching. Kids who whinge all through the supermarket, eternally grateful. I'm thinking of emigrating to Greenland.

At least there will be no Ebola.

Constantly changing law

By Surloin Steak | Published: October 12, 2014 | Edit

Swamped with an ever increasing number of commands.

The same bunch of pip-squeaking self-seeking do-gooding toe-rags.

Laws which strangle our liberty and infect our thoughts.

An excuse to wrap us in cotton wool and push us around.

Permissible in another age.

The savagery with which *public servants* impose these ephemeral arbitrary rules.

How can any *intelligent* person believe in all that smuck?

Brought to Justice

By Rumplestiltskin | Published: October 11, 2014 | Edit

What a curious and misleading phrase that is. Brought to Justice! As if one were bringing a deserving case to an actual, real or tangible thing.

Let's bring the scapegoat to 'justice.'

Let's take the one responsible for everything which we find unacceptable to the *Inquisition.*

I've never heard of anything so ridiculous in my life!

Slavery

By Lawrence van Der Splurgen | Published: October 9, 2014 | Edit

If anyone thinks slavery has been abolished then they really don't understand human nature. They need to look again. What could be finer than to tell another human being what to do? Mankind is hierarchical by nature. Slavery has always been around and it always will be. It's actually on the increase (A close relative of mine is adamant that the rest of the human race were created to serve her, and her alone).

Parliament makes slaves of us all. It interferes in all our daily lives.

As we are reeled slowly into a Police State organisations with 'received authority' pry into everything we do.

Today the **Ebola** virus has made its way across the Atlantic and into the United Kingdom. Why do European Governments always have to interfere? What's wrong with indigenous Societies taking some responsibility for their own welfare?

The planet is already saturated with selfish, violent, fatuous anthropoids.

DECAY is really just a natural way of trimming back the rising population.

COMMENTS

No shorts or laces

By Sarin | Published: August 27, 2014 | Edit

What a disgrace to the Asian community! Once again young Muslim men have been sent to prison for having sex with even younger white girls. Something which has been going on, I believe, for countless centuries. Many have been accused of rape, when it is clearly not (the law having been changed so that any physical contact at all with someone aged thirteen or younger can be classed as rape). These young women didn't need to:

- Get in the car
- Take money and bribes
- Flaunt themselves along the kerbside
- Willingly have sex

Why this obsession among the hypocritical British media and Social Engineers working for the Government. Could it possibly be something to do with that three letter word again, and the sale of news?

In most Muslim countries it is normal for older men to marry younger women.

In *Great* Britain it is now *normal* to have same-sex marriages.

And who is going to be made a scapegoat for the bad parenting, absent fathers, and loose women?

Are we still allowed to speak the truth without a backlash from the herd?

Go on then,

Sack me!!

Wonderful Land

By Lawrence van Der Splurgen | Published: August 24, 2014 | Edit

TODAY'S NEWS

More than enough Members of the Vice squad invaded the home of pop legend Sir Cliff today in a bid to root out every scrap of personal memorabilia they could find. Friends in the media were tipped off well in advance even though Sir Cliff has not been charged with any crime. It has been suggested that he may have asked a bachelor boy where the nearest *public convenience* was nearly thirty years ago.

On to other news:

Israel launched yet another missile attack on Gaza completely destroying an apartment block containing many families and children. The British Government will continue to supply military aid to the area and indulge in 'talks.' The Ebola outbreak is now worse than ever. We could be hit by an asteroid at any moment. President Putin has had his convoy of lorries reversed.

Those responsible for shooting down flight MH17 have been acclaimed as war heroes.

Comments

British heads will roll

By Usuli Twelves | Published: August 21, 2014 | Edit

Why shouldn't we fight for our beliefs?

Grey headed gull seeks refuge

By <u>Sarin</u> | Published: August 18, 2014 | <u>Edit</u>

Not long to wait now.

The grey headed gull will be flapping its wings again.

I wonder what they have been feeding it on to make it looks so well?

£7,000000

Coronation Street: return of boring Ken Barlow

By <u>Lawrence van Der Splurgen</u> | Published: August 12, 2014 | <u>Edit</u>

Intelligent. Compassionate. Understanding. Those are the words I would use to describe Bill Roache. It could all have been so different.

Another jury another day another verdict: the pigs rolling out of the Courtroom gleaming from ear to ear and their *porksman* muttering: "Bill Roache was a predatory paedophile. We have never seen anything so shocking in our life."

"The entire force is greatly relieved that such a dangerous individual is now safely behind bars."

We weren't treated either to the much hogged phrase: "Jekyll and Hyde character," until Rolf Harris appeared in the dock.

Nor were we able to see the poor ruined 'victims' swaying away with their bags of loot.

Any Comment?

Famous actor dies today

By Usuli Twelves | Published: August 12, 2014 | Edit

NO COMMENT

Don't make me laugh Mr Cameron

By [Lawrence van Der Splurgen](#) | Published: August 9, 2014 | [Edit](#)

Dear *'Listening* Prime-Minister,'

Do you think you will ever be able to *combine* insatiable lust for power with a desire to curb the long **snouts of the law?**

They would even give Professor 'Ambrose' Scrivens (Church elder at the Jubilee centre) a run for his money.

Can you see any contradiction at all between your Hippocratic Oath and the numerous wars you have gleefully supported? The next time you are giving your backing to the big-wigs in the **legal industry** spare a thought for the ordinary man in the street who has to live with their ridiculous game of charades. Never travel in a tin can by the way.

Turkish men By [Sarin](#) | Published: August 1, 2014 | [Edit](#)

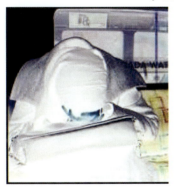

I decree that all Turkish men should in future:

• smile more often

• quit urinating in the street

• remain faithful to their wives

Failure to abide by these rules will result in a seven hour reading of the *Koran.*

Had their asses kicked

By Lawrence van Der Splurgen | Published: July 31, 2014 | Edit

Well, who would believe it?

The pigs were drooling all over the Court room steps.

Rolf Harris will not have his 'unduly lenient' sentence increased!

Advice to Putin

By Usuli Twelves | Published: July 31, 2014 | Edit

The Shed

By Lawrence van Der Splurgen | Published: July 29, 2014 | Edit

That's not a place I am familiar with but I have heard a lot of bad things about it.

I have heard

By Sarin | Published: July 28, 2014 | Edit

I have heard that in Great Britain people can be evicted from their homes and turfed out on the street just for complaining about a bit of damp on the wall.   Private Housing Associations don't even have to give a reason (clause 21).

So much for a fairer society Mr Cameron.

Isn't this all about labels?

The shed by the way had its brackets ripped off at the weekend.

Looks as if someone is conducting a vendetta.

MADMAN ON THE LOOSE!

The Complainer

1 under every bed

By Lawrence van Der Splurgen | Published: July 27, 2014 | Edit

On the pretext of hunting down every scrap of kiddie porn the Authorities have managed to get even more snooping powers and control of the Internet. The Internet started out as a forum of free expression.

It's becoming more and more difficult to express your opinion without being spied on and reported to the Smegs, who have their own version of what is right and wrong.

Any Comment yet?

Rapist Judge

By Lawrence van Der Splurgen | Published: July 27, 2014 | Edit

I saw the Judge being harassed outside his home for falling asleep in Court as if he had murdered or raped someone. Still, it makes a change from one of those idiots reprimanding an ordinary member of the public for spitting.

The man in the dock had been charged with 'rape.'   He must have accidentally brushed against her school skirt: well, that's all it takes these days for someone to be charged with a serious sex crime.

Incarceration for poor parenting

By Lawrence van Der Splurgen | Published: July 27, 2014 | Edit

The control obsessed Government now wants to put parents who don't make sure their children go to school in prison (if there are prisons, then they need to be filled!).

How do you make a teenager who doesn't want to go to school, who sees it as an indoctrination centre, obsessed with controlling and brainwashing, do what you tell them? Parents can be sent to prison for striking their child. You can't make someone go to school if they don't want to. If certain schools were more User friendly then perhaps pupils who found the whole experience boring would get a lot more from their time there.

Do one Mr Cameron!

Mutilation of the Generals

By Sarin | Published: July 26, 2014 | Edit

My recent application to work as Surgeon to the high and mighty has been rejected.   I am most upset. I already had my 'Shipman' medical bag at the ready.

What really plebbed-me-off was seeing the Ukrainian dissidents scouring the crash site with their Tesco bags full of jewellery. I thought I could see a pair of knickers hanging from one plastic bag. In the midst of the wreckage I caught sight of a plain clothes Officer taking photos of all the men. He and the rest of his cronies were sifting through the debris to see if they could find anyone's mobile phone.

It's okay for the Plebs to read people's messages. They do it all the fking time!

Mayhem on the West Bank

By Lawrence van Der Splurgen | Published: July 26, 2014 | Edit

All political parties are interested in power and wealth. Their ambition is to rule. If the Palestinians had half a chance they would blow Israel all the way to Mars.

It is not unnatural for kingdoms to go to war.

New Snooping Laws

By admin | Published: July 10, 2014 | Edit

Let me know your views on the new snooping laws and what ever happened to Nick Clegg the Liberal.

End of Free Speech!

By Sarin | Published: July 6, 2014 | Edit

With Jihadists flying in increasing numbers to wars in the Middle East the Government are trying to pounce on any stray messages on Facebook, or other Social networking sites, in the hope of stifling free speech. Surely Muslims should be allowed to fight if they want to? What is wrong with them communicating with like-minded individuals? Not everyone believes in the British Imperial idea of peace and bulls-bollocks.

Millipede tells the truth

By Surloin Steak | Published: November 19, 2014 | Edit

It's rare to hear a Politician speak the truth. It could well mean the end of their political career.

However, I did hear Ed Miliband say today that;

'Conservatives are only interested in people with money. If you are poor they don't want to know."

Girl Guide movement

By Surloin Steak | Published: November 19, 2014 | Edit

Politics has now entered the innocent and odoriferous camp site of the Girl Guides with demands we quit judging any fat ugly dykes on the extent of their physical attractiveness. This is blatant 'sexism!'

Hey, where are the **new laws** to prevent any further acts of discrimination?

When we get acts of Parliament to tackle this kind of thing it must be time to shut up shop and emigrate to the North Pole chaps.

A Lady member of the Conservatives remarked about the behaviour of some MPs:
"They need to stop shouting. It doesn't look good!"

Contempt of Court

By Lawrence van Der Splurgen | Published: November 18, 2014 | Edit

Have you ever heard of anything so ridiculous?

These people are so far up themselves…

Everyone knows the law is an ass.

If it was up to me I'd have them all lined up against a wall and forced to listen to *Harriet Harman.*

Incitement to hatred

By <u>Sarin</u> | Published: November 18, 2014 | <u>Edit</u>

First of all, if I do want to express a deeply primitive emotion then I will do. Okay! I don't need permission. I don't have to get down on my hands and knees to some high and mighty female bishop with a penchant for all things African, queer, coon, or feminist. If I want to conduct a campaign against thieves, Italian waiters or warthogs I will do, and it's no business of yours unless you want some.

How can you legislate against an opinion?

Actually, 'hate' is a bit too strong. Perhaps detest, despise or dislike is enough. If it 'destabilizes' society, then **too bad**!

Tory radicalisation

By <u>Rumplestiltskin</u> | Published: November 17, 2014 | <u>Edit</u>

What could be more radical than a policy of bullying and intimidation towards any doctrine different to your own. Keep the faith, bro!

Raising the dead

By <u>Surloin Steak</u> | Published: November 14, 2014 | Edit

How can you possibly *prove* something which happened twenty months ago, let alone thirty or forty years ago? It's hard enough to *prove* something which happened only yesterday. Why are the control freaks and twisted moral head-hunters so hell bent on tracking down nonconformists, if it isn't for loot and a nice big pat on the back from Big Brother?

♦ It may just come down to a few slender bullet points:

Jagger's confidential records

By Surloin Steak | Published: November 14, 2014 | Edit

I've been saying for years that doctors are far too willing to hand over so-called 'confidential' information at the drop of a hat. Why can't they just be honest?
Get it through your thick skulls. We're not stupid: there's no such thing as 'confidentiality!'

Tiger seen in Paris

By Surloin Steak | Published: November 14, 2014 | Edit

Don't these people know anything. Big cats have been spotted roaming the countryside for hundreds of years. They belong to the 'phenomenal' world and don't exist in conventional time. A bit like a ghost.

Julien Blanc

By Rumplestiltskin | Published: November 14, 2014 | Edit

Does anybody really need lessons in how to pick up girls?
What really worries me is the speed with which the Government blocked his entry into the country. Aren't we all free to have an opinion.
Why do people in the Establishment have to make theirs legally binding on everyone else?

Filthy rodents

By Rumplestiltskin | Published: November 14, 2014 | Edit

With the rat population beginning to outnumber us two to one, isn't it about time we did something to get them off our backs?
What kind of creature wants to be a cop, Magistrate, or Judge anyway?

Bodies in the street

By Rumplestiltskin | Published: November 12, 2014 | Edit

Why should a tiny little country like Great Britain be so interested in sticking its nose into another country's internal affairs. Why should we be so concerned about "desperately ill" people who are totally unconnected to us in a completely different part of the world?
Oh, bring the dead bodies over here then! Let's see how fast the virus spreads.

No way out

By [Rumplestiltskin](#) | Published: November 12, 2014 | [Edit](#)

It is actually more difficult to get out of the country than to get in. Police forces throughout the United Kingdom are stealing passports in an effort to control everyone and prevent them from escaping abroad. Other travel documents are also seized so that they can reduce the amount of crime in other parts of the world. And they said that *British Imperialism* was dead.

Bomb disposal Wardens

By [Rumplestiltskin](#) | Published: November 12, 2014 | [Edit](#)

Pressure is growing to send more bomb disposal wardens quickly to the Middle-East and other imminent war zones. The new Wardens have been specially trained to clear mines from roadways, parks and alley ways. They will be armed with the new detectors developed by O'Malley.

Anti Social behaviour

By [Sarin](#) | Published: November 9, 2014 | [Edit](#)

Anti Social behaviour is now classed as a serious mental illness for which you can be incarcerated. Society is being saturated with delinquents who display a flagrant disregard for their enemies.

How to pick up postage stamps

By [Surloin Steak](#) | Published: November 9, 2014 | [Edit](#)

You have to be careful when attempting to pick up postage stamps in case you hurt their feelings or go too far. It will simply not do to smooth talk them into bed either. Far better to concentrate on making detonators.

Tory bootlickers

By [Lawrence van Der Splurgen](#) | Published: November 13, 2014 | [Edit](#)

After several attempts to get a response from the Tory party and its Generals on a wide range of subjects such as police harassment, the suppression of free speech, increased surveillance and monitoring of citizens, I decided never to bother with them again.
With an election looming you can bet they will be greasing round every influential voter they can to get back into power.
I wonder just how many dirty tricks they will employ to get rid of UKIP>>>

Doomwatch

By Usuli Twelves | Published: November 6, 2014 | Edit

It emerged today that the Security services (M15) are allowed to view all **information passing between a Lawyer and their client**. Yet again the Authorities are being granted more powers to intrude into people's private affairs. What happened to innocent until proved guilty?

Christian martyrs

By Sarin | Published: November 6, 2014 | Edit

Two Christians have been murdered in Pakistan for desecrating a copy of the 'Koran.' I burn a bible every day and nobody does a damn thing.

Yabba yabba yabba

By Usuli Twelves | Published: November 30, 2014 | Edit

Does anyone think that Celebrity versions of 'the Chase' quiz show are fixed? It seems much harder for ordinary members of the public to win anything, yet alone £120,000. I would like to see Big mouth Woss appear on Mastermind and look so impressive. Oh, I knew the answer to that one. How amazing, how unexpected...

Would have killed Saville

By Surloin Steak | Published: November 27, 2014 | Edit

The journalist and broadcaster Michael Buerk admitted on Celebrity **Big brother** today that he would have killed Jimmy Saville if he had known what he did. Buerk by name, buerk by nature.

GOVERNMENT LACKEYS INC.

By <u>Lawrence van Der Splurgen</u> | Published: November 10, 2014 | <u>Edit</u>

Low IQ?
Can't spell?
Small penis?
Don't suffer in silence.
Join the Met!

- Free eye test
- Company car
- Strong pair of handcuffs
- Arrest on sight
- Gather false information
- Always be in the right
- Bully intimidate and condemn
- Share kiddie porn
- Access to firearms
- take advantage of new recruits
- impute the weak and vulnerable
- bludgeon protesters
- Gang logo
- Interfere with DNA samples
- Pillar of the Establishment
- Early pension rights
- Grooming facilities
- Private Indoor Cinema
- Personal arrest warrants
- Membership badge
- Snooping certificate/s
- Photographic library
- Stalking guide
- Harass dissenters
- Bend the rules to your convenience

No bad individuals allowed
Entry qualification as standard
Excellent rates for fiction writing

Dear Factotum,
Could you please pass on my message to Mr Simpson.
I don't know who else to appeal to.

Dear Mr Simpson,

I am writing to you again about the disruptive and intimidating nature of the police harassment I have been receiving for years.

Once again they turned up at my home demanding to be let in (or they would get a warrant) so that they could go through my home, clambering into all my personal spaces, checking all my bags, looking in my wardrobe, scrutinizing all my private thoughts, snooping through my laptop, demanding I tell them who my girlfriend was, asking me all about my private life, looking at all my private letters and photographs.

They sit down as if they own the place with a smug smile on their face while the neighbours gossip outside the window. I keep telling them to leave me alone but they keep turning up out of the blue, making me poorly and extremely annoyed for days.

I told them again today that my original offence was contacting my ex partner on the phone, on one day, nearly five years ago, and that it was neither malicious nor threatening.

Last month I applied for a new passport. I wasn't intending to go anywhere, but wanted to use it for *identification.* They turned up to arrest me because I had not taken it in to be registered at the Smeg-centre. Last year they arrested me after I had forgotten to log off at the Central library and threatened me with five years in prison. Then they had to let me go.

My partner was at her wits end today worrying they were going to take me away if there were any signs that I had tried to look for my ex partner (who left with all my property) on my computer (we broke up because I did not desire her). Thankfully I am not that stupid.

I am a Writer and Artist. They took copies of all my work with them. They downloaded all my work onto one of their memory sticks. What has the Members of Parliament in this Democracy been doing to allow them such unhindered access to our private thoughts and space?
This cannot go on. Who can help if not a Member of Parliament.

They turned up at the end of my sentence for the phone call business and told the Magistrates I was a dangerous Sex-Offender who would try and rape my ex partner or a member of the public. When I stood up for myself and said it was "Absolute rubbish!" I was accused of being 'aggressive.'

If something serious happens as a result of their on-going harassment then it will only be the fault of the Government. I am sure they are interfering in my e-mails, blocking some of them from being sent, and obtrusively examining my mobile phone.
What on earth is going on in this Country?
Incidentally, the Creators of the Internet wanted it to be about 'Freedom.'

Yours Sincerely,
Mr Y.D. Ibother
PS I would appreciate a reply on this occasion, if only to say you have read my letter.

Colin rang

Colin rang me a few moments ago.

I must say, I am getting a bit sick of him stalking me, but today it was about something really important.

He said that he had come by something which would completely change the way I looked at him.

I have ten minutes to finish eating my supper, put the cat out, go to the bog, and see to Rosemary...

Then I have to shoot over to the club. He is going to meet me on the steps.

I hope it's not about the boil on the back of his neck again...

When I arrived at the Wheel tappers and Shunters on Manningham Villas he was sweating profusely and could hardly get a word out. He took me inside and led me down a dark corridor. I could hear a band playing. It was something by Acker Bilk and his jazzmen.

Looking shiftily to the right and to the left he fitted the key in the lock and opened the door to the Snooker hall.

"I have the item tucked away in a drawer!" he blurted.

"I don't want anyone else to find it!"

He sprung open the drawer, and my jaw dropped.

"You swine!" I said.

"Do you mean to tell me that you have brought me all this way to show me a Playtex bra?"

He looked quite relieved, and sat down on a chair, patting his forehead with a handkerchief.

"Where did you get it?"

"You haven't been raiding Fern Britton's washing-line again?"

Colin nodded towards the wardrobe. One of the doors was half open. Inside I could see what appeared to be a pair of lady's nylons and a Nurse's outfit.

"How long has this been going on Bob, I mean Colin...?" I sighed.

"Do you mean to tell me that this is what you were up to all the time we were in assembly or having a snipe behind the Headmaster's back in the staff room?"

Colin began sobbing and started to look very distressed.

"Please don't tell Sylvia," he pleaded. "This is going to be the very last time. I can't afford to take any more chances."

We could hear footsteps coming down the corridor.

Colin hurriedly shut the drawer, and I went to stand in front of the wardrobe. The door was flung wide open, and who did we see standing there in the doorway, but Stan Collymore.

He pointed to Colin, who was red faced and doing up his laces.

"If I see you in here again!" he said. "I will ban you for life!"

"This is not something which should be happening on the premises." I pleaded on Colin's behalf.

I said he had always been first on parade, with a previously unblemished record.

Just then Colin let out a loud bark, and raced towards the fire-exit. We tried to stop him but he was too fast for us.

Before you could say 'Bobs-your-uncle' he was clattering down the steps and out into the street.

We were too late to stop him jumping into the river.

He dived in fully clothed and then disappeared under the water.

I could hear the sound of the river barge as it came upstream.
As the barge drew nearer the spot where Colin had plunged in the
water started to froth, and something totally unexpected darted out.
It looked like a large lobster or crayfish.
It crashed against the hull of the barge throwing everyone overboard.
Then I saw Colin appear above the surface once more.
He was waving something in his hand.
I turned round and stormed off in disgust.

Perhaps he had imagined the girl, the compartment, the
transvestite, and the Basque separatist?

With the shame of a shaman he loitered on the
starboard side for times without number while the
wadding tick-tocked down the stretch.

Aspiring for the restitution of his 'X' ray vision
the *railwayman* could hear the shunter through the
laminated bog glass as he noisily uncoupled the
locomotive in two. But his mind was in a quagmire and
he had drunk the last tango. Beast of the boulevards.

Only as the vehicle accelerated out of the station
did the idiot finally saddle his hinny.

Secure in the bare supposition that he had probably
preserved his nefarious freedom F. emerged from the
W.C. and cracked his forehead in disgust.

As they began to gain speed he could clearly discern
the rear portion of the express receding under the
canopy...with his camera, his bucks, and every single
one of his travel documents asking to be looted.

Poker-head turned to find everyone left on board
frowning with conjecture in his direction.

Milked his freedom for all he was worth...!

> 'On swift sail, flaming.
> From storm and south.
> He comes, pale vampire,
> to my mouth...'

His old ticker...

The rain started to lance more saliently, when they noticed the spooks clambering slowly up the pass. The Big-people were arguing about a man who had looked at her in the Shoulder. A car headlights dazzling the pattern hurried him back in the refuge.

Almost immediately he came creeping up the stairs, grinning wildly, with Mary snapping like empty thunder.

Her body bounced like a golf ball as it ricocheted down the steps to every steady thump of their heart.

"The 'Bogeymans' gonna getchya! The 'Bogeymans' coming up to getchya!" Danny jibed as he came staggering into their room clothed in ebony, and swiftly cracked on the switch.

The terrified beings vellicating in the swaddling pretended to be hard on.

Like a *private detective* he carefully inspected the bedroom carpet, feeling over the course woollen matress on his hands and knees with the expertise of a craftsman. Danny was up to his armpits in nicotine. The man in the moon had a gleam, and should have been fast asleep...

"Have you been out of bed, have you?" he

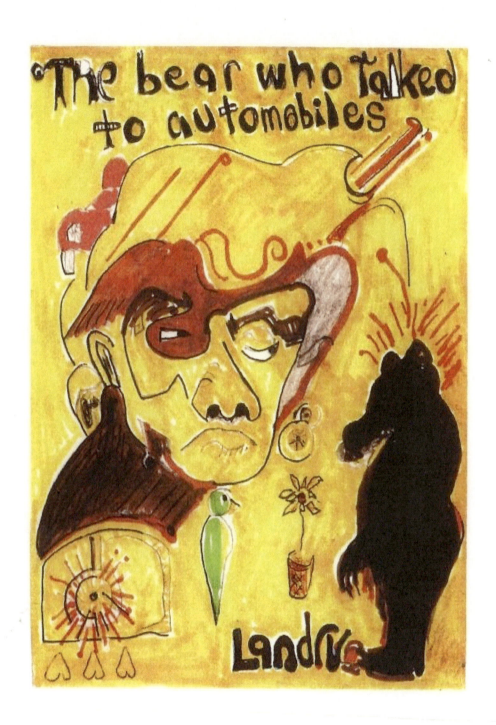

THUNDERBUCK RAM ARTWORK

"Don't your Inspectors ever check the registers except when I'm on duty? Why is there always damage to the Signalbox apparatus after each shift that *the Spiv* has been in harness?"

The Mayor screamed and packed his briefcase. "How dare you try to tell me how to operate the schedules!" he barked dogmatically. "It's not the position of subordinates to go beyond their stations." Stalker glared like a doomster.

"I've got a son of ten at home who could run a Signalbox without any trouble," he sneered. "What's important is to have individuals who are accountable. I am convinced that you are not a fit and responsible person to be left in charge of running a *Shit-tip*," he scoffed. "And don't give us any of your clever clap-trap either. Anybody can learn the process parrot fashion if they wanted to."

"Not if they had a speech impediment!" sparked the Flash. "What about my signatures of support?" he quaked. "There are mutants who have worked with me in excess of five years who are willing to testify that I am able to cope with the most critical emergency situations, and who have said in writing that they have every faith in my abilities."

Stalker whispered behind his upheld hand to indicate the deposition had been long overdue. They stood from the bench in unison ready to march him out of their sight.

"Concerning the correspondence with my Member of Parliament?" he interceded. "Wasn't Jones failed on his rules and ejected from the *terminus* after fourty years in the grade, and reduced likewise. He resigned three weeks later and relinquished his life-pension. You informed my M.P. that I derailed a passenger train and painted a distorted picture of mayhem! How am I ever expected to escape this noxious persecution to a saner branch of humanity? Mustapha can wriggle out of anything."

223

Danny assured him that it would be better along the chevron by the cherry orchard. The wind blasted through the roots of his hair and made his cheeks go cold. The iron horse brayed with a shovel-full of sparks.

A lorry reversing blindly into the main road from the knacker's yard knocked them clean off their pedestal. The bike slid onwards across the tarmac and connected with a lamp-post...

"I'm terribly sorry," admitted the chap. "It was all my fault!"

He was a bag of nerves and was full of remorse, but who would volunteer the compensation?

"Accidents will happen," said Danny grimacing. He stubbornly remounted his motorcycle with a deep gash gushing its gravy down his leg. Mathew's wound was insignificant in comparison. But still they didn't need an operating theatre.

The Ulsterman adamantly refused to charge for any treatment.

14

He left the quacks on Church street with his prescription and trotted through the yard along the crowded shopping precinct to the *Apothecary*. He ducked in an alleyway when he saw Moran halting down the hill.

The attender was a beautiful girl with blonde hair who smiled at him as he glowed like a morning lantern.

On Saturday there were at least six assistants working behind the counter as he handed in his note.

His cream dome perspired like a windscreen as he appeared to be examining a shaving stick.

They each took it in turns to examine the contents on the pad. "Do you know what this is used for?" they giggled. "We've never heard of that brand before."

Flash explained once again that *Supersod permanent lawn replacement* was a new 'wonder drug' from the States which was supposed to cure his congenital 'deformity?'

To prove his point he held up the advert which Esmerelda mark 2 had recently posted.

But they didn't seem to click on...until customers began surveying his summit in the queue.

His face began blistering as Moran gandered against the door-glass.

After six months of pate-wetting the villi hair had still not begun to show signs of curding.

F. sheltered nervously beside the stack of featherlite while the senior chemist answered on the fax. "You'll have to wait one moment!"

Behind the counter *Amini* touched her up. She glared obnoxiously toward the hairless article. What a bloody cheek! Who on earth wants to hear from you!

The red-head passed him a mystery bag containing the magic lotion with a solemn expression as he dispensed ninety pounds cash into their till.

The other hosts loitered curiously over his scalp. As he reached the door the entire staff burst out laughing in giltish titters.

334

Gliding lugubriously by the supervisor's mess the bedraggled Flash was just about to slink down to the sidings when he heard a familiar voice ring-out from the sentry catch.

"Hey there, *Bald Eagle*!"

"What the hell are you doing down in this neck of the woods?" vituperated the 'Flying D.'

His wild expression gradually subsided to a calmer ocean.

"Visiting relatives," he gulped. "Did you earwig about Katie's initial suttee?"

==============================

The 'subdued' 'Flash!' taking the bread, and broke it and said. "Take this and eat; this is my body!"

'How do you hold a 'moonbeam' in your hand?' Parting is such sweet sorrow...

He finally got his 'end-away.'

The copy-cat filler smeared her super-sternal crotch!

"I love you, I love you, but the world grew too hot!"

"He'll never go to heaven now! You know it's a SIN to look at girls!"

"Oh, he'll get over it!"

Seemed a bit short for breath though...

If a small fish wants to survive it has to tell the *fisherman* where the big fish are hiding.

But it's later than you think my friend...that was very pusillanimous of you.

Dick *Ebola* spyed in her bedroom!

==============================

333

FOREWARNED

quem tu quasi lubet, ut lubet, moveto
quantus sies, uti sis foris paratus

Catilina 2.50 B.C.

How To Correctly Insult a *Milesian* Woman

This book is a statement on the demise of innocence, and a swipe at the bog-trotter's two-faced palter of lies, where vengeful Eros degenerated into vice;

The truth should, forgive the expression, 'all hang out,' as an enchiridion of contemporary Scylla and internecine conflict, where 'to censor nothing is an act of love'...

'This' deviant desire, which turns to bastard beauty, invokes the *Judas kiss of morality* above the jesuitry of 'human rights,' inherited from discredited ideals, to energize the pioneer spirit in our flying man to higher and greater 'deeds of disorder;' to baldly Odyssey where no bird has flown before, emplaned by the sudra's lust for punishment, whose inner chord recalls *its* wayward beast, and then feasts on the carrion. For even fickle Ge must teen, that 'wolf' within the human mollusc will lead to 'strife' outside the home.

But this sucked orange 'caste' which shanghai's an increasingly powerful sex drive cannot invoke at any particular whim in time, by the 'divine right of government,' through its mutant benchmen and *Daanite-President*, proclaiming as a pit of abiding folly the childlike error of free will, the double-headed Cyclops of crime and punishment.

The Swarm's hierarchy of industrious establishment puppets, who are the *actual* foul Scythians in all of this; looting like leeches on the active artery; the parasite 'equality;' a strangulating hernia raping the function of emuete, whose whore surgeons of the retrospect distil sentences pathetically from one to another, as their contrivance interferes with an absolute necessity; *will provoke them to passion.*

Didn't an old world prophet once Ko that; 'he who is without guilt let him cast the first stone?' Or as the North American Indians used to account 'do not judge a man until you have walked a mile in his moccassins,' and since 'no rat crosses the same river twice.'

Yet as the moment of impact we *l'agents de provocateur*, painting with the brushstrokes of our words, are under attack from tellurian hellcats and crusading Amazons, who would castrate us in a jar of moralic acid, if fortune favoured them.

If we are indeed *to judge a host by its cook*, then I can only urge the *Outlaws* to turn the board and wreck the table.

If the Clansmen laud to the skies are a thorn in your side, then be an a dart in their tribunal gut; become what you are, burst the chains of your imprisonment and play the starring role; as a *Battering Ram* to wooden laws and castle gates. Realize your fondest rain to fertilize our *horrida bella* between the sky and the earth; and reassert hyperion influence in the Universe. Overthrow the widespread perjury of the masses who would steal our assimilate thunder and rob us of the golden dawn to come; learn *'how to correctly insult a Milesian woman!'*

However, if you are of the people, run for the larder, little spider, I am about to switch on the light!

Landru   Dublin: March 1989

He had something to show her down on the pig-run.
She was always stuffing her mouth with grubs so no
wonder she was consistently riddled with worms.

Mathew collected all of them together, and began
their mid-day *banquet*.

His mother felt cause for concern, but decided not
to say anything since he was managing so peacfully.

Annabelle, Golliwog, Jemima, Raggy doll, and Teddy
bear were each lovingly fed *cream and honey* by the
sensitive young lad.

He lifted them soberly from the cardboard budgerow
he had fashioned, and circumstantially attended their
apparel in a manner which was totally blameless.

Browsing on the bristle doormat he tenderly brushed
their unkempt filaments, administering to their every
need and packing them neat in the box.

As the lemon flare sparkled serenely through the
fecund hatchery, touching the brass plateframe, he
smoothly cradled his special resolve swaying in his
arms, before laying her down along the rail.

Mary froze in the threshold with the remains of
the baking bowl oscillating in her fingers.

Suddenly, as if from nowhere, a black figure stood
in the doorway, blocking the sunlight from his vision.

"He hadn't heard anyone clambering over the leather!"
Danny's towering shape burgeoned on the step with
his brawny nippers resting against the door reveal,
the stink of the 'Shoulder of Mutton' still reeking
on his breath...as Mathew, looking up, raised his hand
instinctively to cover his face from the glare, and
the man fired on him with spiteful venom.

Binkie had parted company long since! He stabbed
the Woodbine on his shield. No chance licking the
bowl out now! The clown had another think coming.

"What's this little *bastard* doing in *my house?*" he
cried, swaggering to sequest his wife with mock
astonishment. Then his pique settled on the comic
muse caught napping.

19

"And what party is this you say?" he'd baulk after a few moments pause, determined to uncover her true allegiance.

Father and son halted at the junction of *Showfield* where the luminous virtue hovered succinctly on its rocky column.

Each passing pair of headlights burst clouds of cotton wool above the rainbow's arch.

His skin-grafts were ridding their fulvous fluid down the bite in his limb but he still insisted on escorting his 'second best' over the uneven length of Hussy street.

With the sensitive hands of a Cyclops Danny held his sons tiny mit like a sublime collector of words. As they trundled slowly past Walter's abode he could see his friend's mother come over to the window. She pulled the curtains of their lanterned room but she did not smile.

At the greenhouse Danny suddenly halted in his tracks.

"Don't forget what I told you my boy," he swished. "Let me hear you once again."

The physically retarded child rehearsed once more his vulgar lines. Practice makes perfect they always say.

"Daddy says that he loves you more than all the pretty birds in the sky and that he'll never love anyone else as long as he lives," repeated Mathew methodically.

He released the grip from his father's stronger brooch and prepared for a showdown with the *Rabbitry*.

But what could this be?

He stammered with grief and his body seemed to shudder under invisible weights. His face seemed mortified with chagrin as the little son wriggled his hand free of pins and needles.

Mathew pored over the great drops of balneation which bounced in disillusionment.

"What's wrong daddy?" he asked. "Have you been peeling Onions?"

67

"Your shirt Moonighan, why haven't you removed your shirt?" she snapped. He was really getting on her nerves that humid afternoon. Point him to the nearest leper colony?

Mathew blushed, and struggled hyper-actively with the hem, while Fatso mimed his attempts to conceal the cynosure of the 'train;' pushing up his bottom lip and nibbling at his gum.

"Titch won't take off his shirt!" he shouted boldly. "Titch won't even take off his shirt Miss!"

"There's no need to be so embarrassed," said Miss Lennon calmly. "All the boys have to...!"

Later in the Orange Canon Holdright came blustering into the stockade wringing his hands zealously in the tinsel centre stage to lobby his prevalent clamour from the cardinal prodigies.

"Good afternoon Canon!" cheered the multitude...he'd already been on the milk round once that tide but he just couldn't stay off the menu.

Beneath the snow white hair his town-crier tongue screed enthusiastically 'twenty to the dozen.' The forthcoming trip to Lourdes. Their imminent First Confession, Holy Communion, and the saving of 'Grace.'

The celibate prattled the parable of the 'Good Samaritan' standing proudly at the vertex of the classroom.

Festering down the front of his dog-collar like a *statue of Baal* he demanded their undivided attention.

His pock-marked clock converted to the intensity of a volcanic eruption when he described how adeptly the Redeemer had transferred the demon into swine, witnessed, of course, by the blessed Virgin.

"We live in the best country in the world!" he stated robustly, "but *even* Catholics can sometimes sin," he lashed.

"I love the little children best of all!" he effused. "Why do they ever have to change into those loathsome adults?"

27

"Always remember Mathew my love," confided the bride of Christ. 'No matter who you are, everyone has a special Guardian Angel who watches over us, and who protects us from any harm.'

"Even when we are tempted to stray from the Roman road the 'holy spirit' leads us back onto the path of righteousness."

She started to examine his face under the rainbow. Had he been stung by a B.? Ariel fell to earth.

"For better or for worse; tell the truth and you will never have anything to fear. Honesty is the best policy! Never be cruel and always be kind."

"Don't worry, my child," she said. "I'll return to see you later. Size isn't everything."

"We're all god's children, and we all have wings."

Nothing seemed to be plain sailing.

When Miss Lennon said it was time for games Mathew had spun around in state of nervous panic.

He had been dreading that moment since dark...and in the confusion he flung off his braces.

"He's taking down his trousers! Isn't he a case?" grinned the buck-toothed red-head near the playing sand.

All the class tittered with beer and skittles. "Only your shoes and vest," hissed the teacher expressly.

What a to-do there was! Swore he belonged on the funny-farm.

Petra Lazzarone threw up his hand longer than a shoplifter's pocket.

Pulling the braces back over his shoulders he tampered self-consciously with the buttons and hung his head in shame.

He trembled as she studied him correctly to see if he would remain upright. Only the best things come in small packages.

The teacher approached to investigate the complaint...

26

Alpha Centauri, with 'golden eyes'

You cloak me in winds
where the secret world spins
and vessels climb storms
above the river's red gorge.

You cover me with flame
where the pageant unfolds
distant ages unborn
on the lava's live rock.

You choke me in blood
which rained from above
whose path beats a hush
from heaven's haughty hub.

You fill me with must
where clouds shift their dust
for my inquisitive eye
from the earth's blue sky.

You find me in stars
where the summer snow falls
on the Argo of fort
among gold doublet glows.

I'll meet you once more
when the plane greets my name
on my happy return
from the light never fades.

Mathew Moonighan
The Holy Family School
May 1967

79

Come away, John

Confucius

I knew him when with hands of hay,
his giant double grinned,
before the fay,
upon his steed,
a halo,
blessed with flame.
Only yesterday, it seems,
the tower,
dressed itself in beads,
to the eyes of beauty,
your eyes turned,
and weighted down,
your undried wings.
Into another skin, the devil drink,
if by another,
your heart weeps,
John in red, Summer-man,
carried high above the clouds.
If no English bullet,
eager for the rising stars,
by thee in green,
Summer man,
pull up the bucket,
from the well of backward rain.
I knew him when,
with hair of grey,
in starch from hillsides deep,
the fair-skinned youth,
Come away John, Come away!

MANGO TREE

-

Strange fruit,

Swinging on a mango tree,

Bruised by stroke of wood,

And the adamant lies of men.

What art thou?

Why do you not fall,

Lingering in the mid day heat,

With your carpet rug open to the wind,

Tied by the neck until you are,

All but eaten.

Mourinho abuse of line staff

By Peter Smith | Published: November 7, 2015

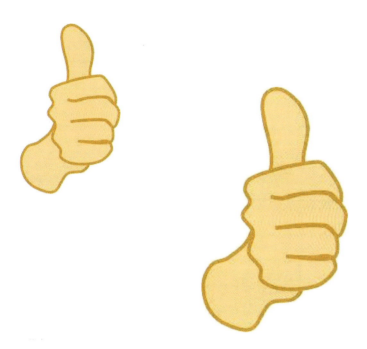

"Out of my way you ignorant peasants.
What a moronic waste of space you all
are. Fuck off the pitch!"

Fastest across the yard

From the air raid shelter
To the wall and back
Walter always won the race.
In short pants and crayons we ran,
In the morning,
The bins alive with orange peel,
And the fizz of wasps.

Walter always won the race,
From the air raid shelter,
To the wall and back,
In the break time sunshine,
With the shadows from St Anne's
Galloping across the bricks,
Gleaming with Autumn yellows,
And the girls screaming like tigers.

From the air raid shelter,
To the wall and back,
Past the empty milk crates,
Glittering on the tarmac,
Falling exhausted on the floor,
And drenched in tears.

As we raced across our yard,
Walter turned, ahead of us,
And waved encouragement,
From the air raid shelter,
To the wall and back,
Full of life, but out of puff,
Rolling all over the ground,
Like fallen skittles,
Resting,
Where we least expected.

Pressing the sheets for Father Peter

With slow and slurring movements,
Father Peter breaks the bread,
Bestowing wine, and blessed we drink.
Into the pantry Sister Clare,
Her feet like summer rain.

I set the board and warm the iron,
Now the guests have gone,
Beyond the Friary walls.

With expert hands she grinds the sheets,
The hard and obdurate fabric of the cloth.
On the side I place her cup,
Beside our garden vase,
Her plain grey overcoat hanging on a chair.

Sister Clare with down-brown eyes,
Gazing,
Listens to my mixed-up words and phrases,
Lisping in her native French,
For hours,
Standing like an angel,
Her perfect form,
And reads my ridiculous note,
Sighing..."Maybe!"
Growing younger by the second.

Murmuring in the light by the window,
Her final words; "Andrew..."
She stepped forward,
And kissed me goodbye.

The mighty brawn of Michael Connolly

There was a lad,
called Michael Connolly,
there was a time,
I knew him well.

I didn't think,
I'd ever want to be,
without his might,
his will, his strength.

I know he could,
I've seen him easily,
bear a truck,
Lift up a dwelling place,
he even stood between me,
and Mullaney,
I miss him now,
like a blue sea.

The bellowing of Allan Tom

Ochre was his hated clock,
woad the ridges of his brow,
red the word-way crammed with chalk,
the pest of every classroom.

They waited till the banging up,
dressed in gloves and whites,
they waited till the coast was clear,
guarding his bright doorway.

Into the hell-hole Brownie leapt,
a hit-man, and a Rapist,
smashing Allan's gawping mug,
into a wheelchair gaping.

A sound like wind a sound so strange,
came blurting from his gully,
spurting from his battered heap,
like a howling genie.

"Who did this to you?" Gaughan asked.
"What a wicked fellow!"
His scarlet face was sheeped in mirth,
skipping 'long the E-wing.

The dog's bollocks

She sings his praises,
every time they pet,
in the Visitor's den,
where her cleavage,
spills,
and his fingers molest the hem of her skirt.

Martin Fungus preens himself in the steely square,
of the cell mirror,
Squirting Clearasil on his flaking skin,
wires of dark hair moulting everywhere,
"You really are the dog's bollocks!" I yelped.

An alien life-form attempted to elope,
from his neck,
His bare arms protruded with a leviathan of blades,
something unpleasant erupted from behind an ear,
"The dog's bollocks!" I said.
"Another innocent man locked up in jail!"
I slapped the desk in disgust.

He stared impassively, like a heap of vanilla,
a nest of love-bites encroaching on his chest,
"Dog's bollocks!" I said.

"Just because I wouldn't give her any more money,
for drugs," he enunciated.
"Bollocks!" I said.
"It'll cost them an arm and a leg when you appeal."
A reptilian leer.

Like a prayer-note in the snow

You are there,
I am here,
it's midnight,
and...
I drink the starlight.

With eyes like two dark beam-holes in the madness.
The wind burning like irons,
the earth turning like fires.

If only skies had been more unbolted,
if only rain had been more loving.

A natural urge while touching

The way I return to you,
here in this prison cell,
Mary.

A microscopic gleam of time,
in Wymondham,
where I was happy.

Like a blissful dolphin, I flew,
jouncing over the waves.

Rarer than foxgloves,
in the depth of winter,
I touched you,
my dear Mary.

Doctors and Nurses

By Rumplestiltskin | Published: December 2, 2014 | Edit

I couldn't help feeling sorry for cancer specialist Myles Bradbury when he received twenty two years in custody for 'touching' boys at his surgery.

Some of his offences happened while the boy's parents were sitting on the other side of the screen.

There has to be a better way to deal with this sort of behaviour than banishing someone into a living hell. Why do sentences have to be so disproportionately high for offences involving sex?

Surely, the loss of his job, home and family should have been enough.

I'm sure he must be extremely sorry and ashamed of his actions.

No-one can help their sexual orientation. It wasn't that long ago *homosexuals* were being sent to prison...

The only people who will be happy with this decision are the Plebs who heard his confession, the prison officers wantonly jangling their keys, and the many warped and twisted individuals awaiting his appearance in their playroom.

There were the usual horrified expressions from the Met.

The justification to continue further witch-hunts against anyone considered different.

Myles Bradbury was hardly a violent and sadistic rapist.

Neither was Max Clifford by the way, who's so-called 'victims' crept willingly to their endeavours. He was right not to apologise.

I have been regularly examined by my doctor "down there" and it has never left me feeling traumatized or dirty.

The most I have ever felt is a slight loss of arousal and mild embarrassment at having my manhood so tenderly handled by a woman I didn't know.

The Ned Kelly memorial banquet

By Rumplestiltskin | Published: December 1, 2014 | Edit

Comments

Riots in Egypt crushed

By Usuli Twelves | Published: November 30, 2014 | Edit

It's only a matter of time until Egypt follows the examples set in Russia and China. When political tyrannies want to suppress free speech all they need to do is issue a command.
The charges of murder against Mubarak are to be dropped. What charges were they?
That he sanctioned the death of ordinary citizens protesting against his regime...
We should feel really sorry for the poor bastard.

School Photographer jailed for taking pictures

By Bird Dung | Published: August 27, 2015 | Edit
When I met with Peabody today he was even more excited than usual.
"You need to BREAK THE LAW TO MAKE THE LAW!" he foamed.
A catalogue of photographs had been passed around the station, with the Director and one or two of the Senior Officers having first shout.
By the time the albums reached him they were already torn, with several of the photographs missing or photocopied.
A Senior Detective said that the Photographer had committed **a serious breach of "trust"** in taking the photographs, but she was extremely impressed by the lengths to which he had gone: many of the snaps were taken from very awkward and revealing angles.

British Government

By Adumla | Published: January 20, 2015 | Edit
What we *really* don't like is people with bigger guns!

Pope says...

By Godfrey Winklebacker | Published: January 20, 2015 | Edit

"We do not need to breed like rabbits to act like responsible parents."
I suppose that's what you get from someone who thinks sex is dirty and will never be the father to anyone but his flock.

Campaign against nudity

By Godfrey Winklebacker | Published: January 20, 2015 | Edit

Bowing down to pressure from outraged feminists and a drop in sales the Sun has decided to scrap its page three model after many decades and are to act like 'socially responsible adults.'

Feminists everywhere are hailing this as a triumph:

"People have been offended by these repulsive images for too long. It's time to cover up, to know what's 'appropriate' and *hide behind-the-veil* of respectability once more. The world has moved on."

"We no longer need to gaze upon the female form as a sexual and artistically perfect creation."

Page three models have been described as "a bit thick," and "lost causes."

We teeter backwards into the black hole of the Dark Ages once more.

Back to the dirty old days of the 'sex-haters…'

The days of the Inquisition are really not too far away.

Why do we always need to be told by the dreary dog-eaten do-gooders in Government what's dirty and disgusting?

It would really be a master stroke if Murdoch only pretended to withdraw the page, and then went back on his word!

* Methinks I will just have to keep my grimy objectionable physique concealed from now on. 😊

POLICE STATE

By Godfrey Winklebacker | Published: January 18, 2015 | Edit

Governments, when they are afraid, will always bring in new laws to cement and hold on to their power. Most Western Democracies are now sliding towards State terrorism and control.

They only want to protect us.

They only want to keep us safe.

It's all for our own good.

Bullshit!

Abu Hamza

By [Godfrey Winklebacker](#) | Published: January 10, 2015 | [Edit](#)

I found him to be a very likeable and amiable fellow without a shred of true nastiness in his bones, but the Home Secretary got her knife in and the Americans wanted a scapegoat.

There was no real evidence, only hearsay, and a kind of 'proof by association.'

If Hitler had won

By [Adumla](#) | Published: January 9, 2015 | [Edit](#)

No Thatcher   No Sadam Husain   No Suez crisis

NO Gandhi   No HIV   No Royal Family

No problems with immigration

No Nelson Mandela   No Ed Balls   No Angela Merkel

No Dimbleby nepotism   No Papacy

No PLO or Israel   No Paris shooting

No Vietnam   No Berlin wall   No Berlusconi

No Wank*r Walliams   No Food Aid   No Band aid

No Stephen Hawking   No Gadhafi

No Anders Breivik   No free speech

No crippling health budget

No Muslim council of Great Britain

No Saudi Princes or Al Fayed

More French attacks imminent

By [Sarin](#) | Published: January 9, 2015 | [Edit](#)

More terrorist attacks are expected in France leading to a heightened level of emergency.

Home Secretary hit by tomatoes

By [Adumla](#) | Published: January 7, 2015 | [Edit](#)
We regret the passing of this ignorant and superficial woman who was totally unable to decide who to trust.

Comments

0 comments

« Why flatfoots are so thick

More French attacks imminent »

Why flatfoots are so thick

By Sarin | Published: January 7, 2015 | Edit

That which an age considers to be evil is just an untimely after echo of what a previous age considered to be good. The atavism of an older ideal.

I don't hate anyone by the way.

Upright citizen

By Sarin | Published: January 7, 2015 | Edit

Our hearts go out to the brave gunman from the States who loyally and steadfastly hunted down members of the New York gang signing them both permanently *off duty*.

Comments

WYMONDHAM: spying and surveillance centre

By Sarin | Published: January 7, 2015 | Edit

Some months ago I sent one of my spivs out to interview a prat from the new Pleb watchtower built in Wymondham, Norfolk. A Representative from the newly established dork colony boasted that their new centre could snoop on anyone within a fifty mile radius and they didn't even need to get up off their lazy asses to do it. He said that this massive new building was erected with the sole intention of gathering intelligence on every single citizen that they could. A room full of monkeys were employed day and night to break the codes of would be transgressors.

Talking about the gathering of intelligence: if a brain cell accidentally fell on the floor or blew through the window I would imagine a massive scuffle ensuing to see who could get their hands on it first.

I'm still expecting the Home Secretary to cave-in to their request to be able to eavesdrop on all electrical devices in the country though. What two word phrase starts and ends with an 'f?'

At her Majesty's pleasure

By Sarin | Published: January 7, 2015 | Edit

Your Majesty,

If they think it will be a worthwhile exercise then let them have their show trial.

Let's see just what crawls out of the woodwork.

During the gulf War we all prayed that nobody would hurt him.

It's all about malice and money.

GERMANY PROTESTS

By <u>Sarin</u> | Published: January 7, 2015 | <u>Edit</u>

Germans protested today that there are not enough Nazi's in the country.

Methinks she protests too much.

Another fawning member of the Establishment

By <u>Sarin</u> | Published: January 7, 2015 | <u>Edit</u>

Why do Solicitors, teachers, and Judges always support the Authorities? Because they are part of the mob, the herd animal man which created the law in the first place.

The attacks have been described as:

AN ATTACK ON DEMOCRACY

AN ASSAULT ON FREEDOM

A BLITZ ON CIVILISATION

France has been described as "hurting."

"These vicious animals have no place in our world!"

Vive le Napoleon!

Vive la Republique!

BUNDERCHOOK ARRESTED BUT RELEASED ON BAIL

By Sarin | Published: January 7, 2015 | Edit

My good friend Doctor *Bunderchook* was arrested around lunchtime on Tuesday and accused of plotting to bring about an end to Western Civilization. A gang of around ten officers, including some in plain clothes (and another twenty on stand-by), appeared in the entrance hall just as he was about to take a lift to the first floor. The good doctor was then bundled into his Apartment where a thorough search was made of his property for any smart phones or internet devices. Dr Jekyll continued to talk about his training methods in an effort to befriend him, while Mr Hyde read him his rights and gleamed like a Cheshire cat. A crowd of onlookers gathered inquisitively on the stairs.

"We always have to do things this way," sniggered Hyde. "You have been marked down as DANGEROUS and our paperwork never lies!"

Two years before while setting up his e-mail account the accused had deliberately typed in his step-father's surname, instead of the one familiar to us all. The matter was reported by his Landlord a few days ago, even though they had been in regular contact since then, and there was no disputing his identity. A box of old business cards was also removed as evidence. Bunderchook tried to remain calm but in the face of so much hostile aggression he paled significantly. He was taken away to be interviewed and denied any *genuine* legal representation. Only a stooge of the Authorities was at hand to guide him towards complete capitulation.

The **legal Representative** had already been scrutinizing his website some days earlier and was full of strange anecdotes.

"They've been dead keen ever since the death of Sara Payne. Great lads. Love every one of 'em." Her face seemed oddly familiar too.

"*What the fk has she got to do with me?*" boomed Bunderchook (or words to that effect), striking the table with the lip of his pipe.

Hyde set the tape rolling and asked him about his *stage-name.* How had it come into being?

A piece of work about a serial-killer written by one of Bunderchook's own students was taken away to be examined.

He was threatened with a long period of incarceration unless he handed over his passwords and gave them unrestricted access to all his personal thoughts, e-mails, and documentation. The *Sow-cubs* had been interfering with his post and photographing him wherever he went for the last five years so this was hardly a shock. Was this new strategy anything to do with him filming their unremitting and noxious persecution. Was the removal of his computer equipment anything to do with their desire to tie his hands and gag his mouth?

If so, it's been a disaster.

Je suis Charles de Gaulle

By Sarin | Published: January 7, 2015 | Edit

Another Muslim attack hits France. The Journalists working at a satirical magazine poking fun at Islam are taught a lesson they will never forget. How long before the same happens here?

God is indeed very great, especially when he is fighting on the side of the European Union.

Ched Evans rapist

By Sarin | Published: January 7, 2015 | Edit

How can anyone settle down to become a productive and law-abiding member of Society if they are constantly hounded by their peers and by the Authorities who simply won't let them forget the past? Ched Evans can't win whatever he says. I'm sure we would form a different opinion of him if we were to hear his accuser *in person*…

Snooping no good for your health

By Godfrey Winklebacker | Published: December 29, 2014 | Edit

The best way to deal with persistent bullies is to pass them a hidden parchment bearing a number of runic symbols.

They'll never know who pressed the button or who gave the command to resist.

COMMENTS

Only yourself to blame

By Lawrence van Der Splurgen | Published: December 28, 2014 | Edit

"Only yourself to blame!"

Take responsibility for your actions.

How many times have I heard this bullshit from members of the Establishment.

So I'm responsible for all the nonsense laws made before I was born, for all the rubbish taught in classrooms, and for the way the mob singles out anyone brave enough and courageous enough to question their rules...Comments

The Metropolitan elite

By Rumplestiltskin | Published: December 23, 2014 | Edit

European heads go to Chancellor for help in solving migrant crisis

By Bird Dung | Published: August 27, 2015 | Edit

Significant new information

By Bird Dung | Published: August 26, 2015 | Edit

I'm not going to name any names, but significant new information has arrived at Bunderchook HQ about the lack of decent sandwiches in the pig's canteen. Just when you thought things couldn't get any worse.

They had all their porky pies left ahead of them.

Review of the Wicker man

By Sarin | Published: February 10, 2015 | Edit

I was seventeen when I first watched 'The Wicker man' and bursting with indignation at the way 'the sacrificial goat' was constantly being thwarted from conducting a *serious criminal investigation.* Just goes to show I wasn't as bloody clever as I thought.

* If they'd waited for the fires to die down a little they could have had a nice bit of *crackling*.

Saint Dominic

By Sarin | Published: February 10, 2015 | Edit

You pay off the maid to avoid a long and embarrassing trial. You decide to pay for the blow job to prevent being dragged to the Penitentiary. What's it to you if a few girls like to party!

There are a lot of envious eyes out there.

You need to be taught a lesson.

I think it's only a matter of time before they get you.

You know these religious types.

By the way. What is 'aggravated pimping?'

Blogger jailed for nothing

By Sarin | Published: February 10, 2015 | Edit

A few years ago during the so-called BlackBerry riots two young men were sent to prison for blogging on Facebook. The pompous moronic fool who jailed them still resides in permanent opulence and is still able to promulgate his ridiculous views to the world.

It's not a matter of right and wrong: it's always been about POWER!

Comments yet

Blessed Ned Kelly

By Godfrey Winklebacker | Published: February 9, 2015 | Edit

We have just celebrated the birth of our most famous bushranger, whose father died in prison for 'unlawful possession' of a *bullock's hide.*
So, the same Judges and assholes were around in those days too…!
We must preserve **law and order** at all costs.
Let's make June 28th a day to remember, and call it 'NED KELLY DAY!'

On-line Asbo

By Godfrey Winklebacker | Published: February 9, 2015 | Edit

New Asbo's are going to be issued to anyone who:
– criticizes or pokes fun at Eskimos
– takes the piss out of people in uniform
– makes any comment deemed as offensive
– writes anything against the State
Everything you write on line will be carefully scrutinized, every word examined, each full stop looked at under a microscope. Anyone found guilty of expressing their views will be gunned down or sent out of the room.

Consolidated power

By Sarin | Published: February 8, 2015 | Edit

Great Britain's philosopher Prince has been opening his large erudite trap again. Charles has been complaining about the actions of Isis. That's the Islamic group trying to conquer parts of the Middle East to set up their own kingdom, with *their own extremist beliefs.*
He doesn't like the way they have been driving indigenous people from their homes, amassing land and taking hostages.
Well, isn't that sad!
Didn't the British do exactly that in Ireland, Scotland, Africa, Palestine, the American Plains and Australia.
Don't these jerks make you want to vomit.
And they're the ones making all the laws, having consolidated all their gains and privileges.

The Metropolitan elite

Authorities like everyone to behave the same.

Authorities like everyone to toe the line.

From childhood authority figures brainwash us never to question authority, never to malign the law, never to question it's supremacy.

When *Elvis Presley* first appeared he was considered to be an extremely dangerous influence. Young people were warned to look the other way. He represented everything which Authority feared most: freedom.

Parents advised their offspring to look towards Cliff Richard for a suitable role-model.

Nowadays we have '**Marilyn Manson**'…

COMMENTS

Perverts: putting them straight

By [Adumla](#) | Published: February 8, 2015 | [Edit](#)

We were required to race across half the country in a war against time.

Bunting was waiting for us on the doorstep. I stole a glance at her dress.

Gumby wheeled the trolley of files from the unmarked pleb-mobile in through the door. I could still taste Anne-Marie on my chops…

"Look, Mrs F. We need to make you aware. Such and such, your former boyfriend is one of the most dangerous sex-fiends in the country. We have been tracking his movements since god knows when."

Mrs. F. was aghast.

"Do you mean to say I have been sharing my home with a dangerous malign and thoroughly nasty Stalker?"

I glanced at Gumby and could not suppress a gleam.

"Here is a catalogue of all his most heinous crimes. There's plenty of statements for you to read through." Bunting fell back in her seat.

"Do you mean to say, someone actually saw his cock thirty years ago? And he wouldn't even let me have a single frigging look in the eight months I knew him!"

Father Murphy

By Peter Smith | Published: February 6, 2015 | Edit

I went to school with a chap called 'Murphy' many years ago. I thought I would just outline a few of his most notable achievements. I know they might be considered quite unusual, but then, none of us are the same, and what is right for one person may not be necessarily right for another…

- had his first sexual experience at the age of four months
- smoked his first joint at two
- at nine he won a Mr Universe contest
- he grew a beard when he was ten
- at thirteen he had already fathered at least six children
- first *royal* at sixteen
- became a grandparent at seventeen
- CSE in woodwork
- caught red handed leaving the Post Office
- first Police Commissioner under 25
- beat female peace-protester to pulp but never charged
- Council leader (prosecuted for embezzlement)
- MI5 operative
- worked as a mole in Public Protection
- ran off with his best friend's fifteen year old daughter

Put down Putin

By Godfrey Winklebacker | Published: February 6, 2015 | Edit
This Russian President will simply not do as he is told.
I'm beginning to think he may be autistic…
For some reason he keeps shifting his position.
Unlike some we could name!

Sad and lonely Glitter

By <u>Godfrey Winklebacker</u> | Published: February 4, 2015 | <u>Edit</u>

It seems to be the ambition of this obsessive and disobliging society to imprison what is now left of the creature known as 'Gary Glitter' until his bones rot and he is nothing more than a slug in the grate.

I watched the former rock star scrambling nervously into court with a large furry hat to keep his head warm and the press clamouring alongside like a bunch of noisy apes.

Whereas I dislike the nature of his offence there has to be a better way to deal with this sort of behaviour than imprisonment. Punishments are so severe that perpetrators commit the most terrible deeds to cover up their crime. It does nothing to improve their life or the life of their victim. It does nothing to encourage them to say they are sorry or to make amends. People are not allowed to move forward with their life or to forget mistakes they made in the past.

My friend 'Sue' was abused by her father. Because she loved him and she didn't want to destroy her family she never reported him. Whereas she became a little frigid her sister turned into a *raving nymphomaniac.*

'Guilt' is something introduced into our psyche by those in Authority.

£ Since my original post Glitter has been found guilty. How he could have been expected to get a fair trial is completely beyond me. You could have brought a random bus-load of students to point the finger at him and the jury would have believed them all. So called 'graphic details' were not released due to their supposed *depravity* (doesn't that amount to 'censorship?').

Governments will have their way no matter what the evidence:

  ✓ careful selection of jurors
     a sympathetic Judge
     verdicts agreed behind closed doors
     manipulation of the media

Captain Ahab's famous last words

By Godfrey Winklebacker | Published: February 3, 2015 | Edit

I saw a poor young man lying in a doorway in the middle of winter yesterday. What he really needed was a hot meal and a roof over his head.

A happy clappy Christian mob approached him like a dead rat.

It could have been snowing.

They probably had the church's reputation to think about.

"Don't you have a home to go to?"

"You shouldn't really be lying there!"

"We'll *pray* for you!"

Just as long as he's not having sex before marriage. It's all they pssing care about.

WHAZZACKS.

Comments

Lady Diana

By Peter Smith | Published: February 3, 2015 | Edit

In my honest opinion I think she was deliberately done away with to prevent the Al Fayed dynasty from having royal connections or am I saying something out of place here?

The Authorities can do whatever they like in the name of public duty.

She'd fulfilled her main duty; to provide a male heir.

Diana was expendable.

Comments

The best part of being rich

By Sarin | Published: February 3, 2015 | Edit

The best part of being rich and powerful is being able to make all the laws which tell others what to do and then being able to do what we like ourselves.

Animal cruelty

By Sarin | Published: February 3, 2015 | Edit

A regular dose of compassion and capital punishment:

- Unnecessary suffering.

- Cruel and despicable acts.

- Hacked to death with no regret or mercy.

This sort of behaviour is endemic in human nature.

Comments

Seven things you didn't know about me

By Godfrey Winklebacker | Published: February 2, 2015 | Edit

1 I lost me virginity at the age of nine

2 I gave Norman Tebbit his alibi

3 I am Prince Harry's true biological father

4 Margaret Thatcher sought my advice about whether to go to war in the Falklands

5 I once worked as a Bobby Charlton lookalike in the World cup final of 1966

6 I hacked into the files of the CIA totally undetected

7 I changed one of Stephen Hawking's nappies

* *Born on 'Groundhog day'*

Word power

By Sarin | Published: February 2, 2015 | Edit

*r*adical   –   one proposing dramatic changes in government

a *rebel*   –   one who fights against those in power

*su*bversive – one likely to overthrow government

*i*nsurgent –   one rising up in rebellion

p*leb*   –   a small insignificant piece of .....

Advice to Murray

By Godfrey Winklebacker | Published: February 1, 2015 | Edit

Need a longer neck.

Bully

By Adumla | Published: January 31, 2015 | Edit

I recall a middle-aged bard named 'Liam' turning up one evening at our writing group. He came to us with the same story on both the evenings he attended. It concerned an airplane landing in a field during the Second World War and the pilots being chased across the mud by a huge steaming red eyed bull…whose name, strangely enough, was 'Bully.'
I told him that the only bullies in this world had their size twelves parked under the desk at the nearest pig wagon.
* I'm convinced he took his story round every writing group in the country.

Boris Johnson

By Godfrey Winklebacker | Published: January 30, 2015 | Edit

How can an albino who is more quirky than a pink eyed Angora in a cement mixer accuse someone else of being a 'loser?'

Comments

The Chase

By Godfrey Winklebacker | Published: January 30, 2015 | Edit

Spot the 'know-all:'

Asperger's syndrome

By Peter Smith | Published: January 28, 2015 | Edit

Yet more funds are needed to avert a crisis in our National Government.

Bilateral aids spending

By Adumla | Published: January 28, 2015 | Edit

Cuts equality
Eradicates poverty
Gives everyone an education
Reduces dependency
Introduces choice over reproduction
Big snout into everything
Wilful misunderstanding
'Justice' instead of 'charity'
Modern day slavery
Right to join a union
Changes to the temperature

Jealousy

By Adumla | Published: January 28, 2015 | Edit

A terrible thing when we have to fulfil our deepest aspirations through the actions of another.

Application for employment

By Peter Smith | Published: January 27, 2015 | Edit

No: Snoops, Alsatians, darkies or Packaderms.

Our libraries

By Peter Smith | Published: January 27, 2015 | Edit

There was an outcry over in bolshy Oxford when it was announced that a library may have to be closed or be supported by private voluntary help. From what I have seen the narks working in libraries have one of the most cushy jobs in the country. Libraries have become one of the most important spying zones in Britain. Citizens are under surveillance from the moment they enter till the moment they lock the door and everything they do is monitored by the State.

UKIP to gain a massive two seats at the General Election

By Peter Smith | Published: January 27, 2015 | Edit

I can see even these predicted seats slipping away if media drones are able to keep up their all out attack and brand them as racists incapable of Government.
UKIP are being pushed out of debates and coverage is being kept to an absolute minimum.

Fishing expeditions

By Peter Smith | Published: January 27, 2015 | Edit

I suppose that would include 'Trawling expeditions.'
All in the name of gathering information on a random ad-hoc basis.
The Security forces must be having a field-day. I can think of no better way to describe this than 'Snooping' on the General public.
'Prying' into all our private affairs.
Royal Mail can be opened and re-addressed because it is 'clearly' in the *public interest.* Every piece of data will be stored on a data-base forever (or until a great big asteroid knocks GCHQ and the CIA right out of the water).

COMMENTS

Ishmael the Poet

I first met Ishmael in the Education department of *Bure Valley Treatment and Indoctrination Centre.* We were doing a course in English and Art History.

Ishmael had a natural aptitude for words and was lightning quick at conundrums. One look at the black board and that was it. His mind juggled the letters quickly into a word before I could even ask who the bloody hell was watching us through the top of the door.

I liked Ishmael from the start even though he looked like a pea on a drum. He was naturally bright and gifted. He was also very generous. I missed him that time he was off sick.

A *brain damaged reptile* (which had been loitering for hours in the corridor) informed us that he had "set fire to his glasses!" and that was why he could not come in to join us for a while.

For two weeks he was absent from our class.

I was overjoyed to see him and extremely impressed when he showed me his first attempt at poetry.

He handed me his poem to read, beaming with pride and enthusiasm. I laughed at the penultimate line…

I think his first poem had a title like 'Why I like beautiful women,' but I will always remember his poem as 'The Rocket.'

'My cock went up like a space rocket…'

I glanced up at the ceiling.

'The Sprats are gonna love this,' I said.

'They'll never let you out in a month of Sundays!'

Council for Civil liberties

By Peter Smith | Published: January 26, 2015 | Edit

Ok. So you are too busy to answer any of my letters.

You don't mind turning a blind eye to police harassment, abuse of police powers, bullying and intimidation. We live in free society?

Pull the other one!

Comments

No food for seagulls

By Adumla | Published: January 25, 2015 | Edit

It has reached the attention of the *coastguard surveillance team* that seagulls have been flying around overhead and trying to 'steal' food. This appalling situation cannot be tolerated for much longer. People living in the area need to be better protected.

Tourists have been 'attacked' by these scavenging marauders from space. No-one is safe from their watchful eye.

It has been noted that the most serious offenders were taking food home for their chicks. *'Repeat offenders'* have been seen loitering on rooftops close to the beach for the opportunity to glut their appetite.

Several scavenging omnivores were observed tearing a portion of fish apart. A small toddler had to run for its life.

Recorded incidents have doubled since the summertime. The birds most at fault were the ones with a blue ring round their shins who seem to have developed a taste for 'Cornish pasties.' Evidence of 'stealing' has been recorded by a specialist team of Observers.

The birds most at fault were the bold urban varieties.

A Government think-tank analyst said that the breed had been ear-marked for study because of their *agility, sharp eyesight, and flight sense.*

Some behaviours were giving greater cause for concern than others.

*Well, they are seagulls for fuk's sake!

Insanity

By Sarin | Published: January 25, 2015 | Edit

When it comes to decision making I would trust an individual to make the right choice over and above that of the deafening herd. Who could be wiser and more in touch with reality? Madness is a rare thing in an individual but when groups get together there is a loud and hysterical clamour.

Among the groups I have singled out for special attention are:

- *the media*
- *Government departments*
- *religious movements*
- *the police force*
- *political parties*
- *the French*

We all know right from wrong

By Godfrey Winklebacker | Published: January 24, 2015 | Edit

Oh, really? You mean we've been brainwashed into thinking we do.

"The problems of the 21st Century are only just beginning."

LANDRU   January 2016

Swapper

Swapper went to school with a marble,

came back with a train-set.

Now he's at the seaside,

wearing cowboy hats.

He's my hero...

Pretty girls and limousines,

six hundred press-ups,

iron railings on the way,

to the white-knuckle-ride.

And laughter round the windpipe.

Blonde bristles,

bare against my throat:

'knocked seven bells of crap,

out of bigger twats than you,

y' spotty faced little prick,'

voice foaming,

like a megaphone,

spitting tampons.

A black eye from the door handle,

mother grinning,

from the bedroom.

Vestibule of light

The black-foot of night had cut and run...

above the window-ledge,

the sun melted like butter.

You sat quite still,

the doors wide open,

like a breath of summer.

Gusts of mistral waft your dampened hair,

thinking how it might have been,

inside the vestibule,

elements of fire,

lie shattered at your feet,

sparkling blue rainbows,

blends of light.

Blushing birds in red and orange,

a frost of sands,

into your chariot racing,

scarlet ribbons,

singing songs you whistle by,

no more,

my grey shadow.

Above the town I'll see you,

in a different light,

time spurred on by seasons,

tiny chunks of glass,

flying by the window,

spiralling to earth.

Smashing the door in

We heard the smash of broken glass,

and then,

the leaded window-frame,

gave in,

two,

screaming fists.

Feet,

pummelling,

The sound of *voices in the door,*

running up the stairs.

Huddled close inside our bed,

me and Genevieve.

Points for the Plebs

Knock knock. Who's there?

You should know the procedure by now.

Where are you from and why are you here?

Dr Jekyll and Mr Hyde?

Who's turn to have the brain cell today?

Please don't let me detain you any longer than is necessary.

Why do you keep coming here. Have you got a cough?

You always remind me of Adolf Hitler.

I find that 'very offensive.'

Kicked anybody's head in this week?

Have you ever snogged a girl?

Here's a copy of the original offence. Phone contact six years ago. Is there something about the truth you don't like to hear.   Why do you keep treating me as if I'm in prison?

Why did you ask me to 'make myself decent.' What's 'indecent' about the human body? Are only cocks mucky then?

I'm beginning to feel a bit like Alfred Hitchcock.

Do you know the way to Amarillo?

Here's a little something for Christmas.

Why don't you leave me alone?

I'm suffering from a bit of dandruff. Would either of you like to recommend a good shampoo?

Try not to trip over the mat on your way out.

Jackson Pollock mattress

Visitors,

welcome to my room,

laid bare for your perusal:

the foam-flecked mattress.

Thrown clear: its shield of cotton sheets.

Observe the t-stained brat-drooled patchwork,

and snow-packed swan-glossed bird-stain.

The manky yawl of shame-faced brushwork,

It's honey-dewed inhuman soil,

The tints soured and turned to jasmine,

Slumped in the seedy gleam of silence.

Behold the golden cockroach

She stood in the House of Commons:

unfit to travel,

not fit to travel,

under arrest.

They were a new breed,

of outcast.

She never sailed rubber ducks

I'm reliably informed,

by the blackboard,

that,

the girl I once knew,

never sailed rubber ducks at lunchtimes.

While I was playing with my train-set,

on the rug in short trousers,

she was not in anyway involved,

never once,

did she,

cross the fields,

and in the lake,

sail rubber ducks during meal-breaks.

Anna Hopka (deceased)

Anna Hopka…

With you coffee jar mouth,

And nails of emerald,

roaring,

Your foot rests below,

Staring blindly,

Calling for more,

On your glasses.

Family photos of wooden,

Cadaverous boxes,

In the loose garments,

Of the secret chamber.

No matter how much you plead,

There will never be a next time.

Walker on the fields of dawn

If mist should cloud the winds of time,
With pools of august red,
From scoundrel hearts in raven coats,
In this crestfallen den…

Lookout for me upon the Land,
With my spirit drum,
Prepare the flowers for April showers,
And sun-drenched drunken seeds.

Even as the morning plane,
Flits from glen to glen,
The cry of gold upon my shoes,
With steam from eagle kings.

A Walker on the fields of dawn,
A Captain of the stars,
If you could hold the one you love,
And magic in your arms.

When the sunrise

When the sunrise,

Melts away the foe of night,

And the morning,

Lends you colours to delight,

Birds of foison float from earth,

Lingering with rosebuds made of gold.

When the sunrise,

Makes the dreams of darkness real,

And the dawning,

Gives you metal curls of steel,

Points of paint-bright feed the land,

Shivering with valour on your soul.

When the sunrise,

Moves your jeweled finger like a star,

And the Chieftain,

Looks down with courage from above,

Whatever deep affection you may have,

Hungering for passion and for love.

GIRL AT THE WINDOW

Where does love begin?

In the window,

In the window,

Where she glances down.

Is she dreaming,

Can she see me?

On her long walk from town,

And down the leaf-wet lane,

Our paths meet,

under the trees,

And she blushes…

Like the figure of David I stand,

In the building,

In the sunshine,

No turning back,

I'm falling,

I'm falling.

For more than one year

For more than a year,

I carried you with me.

For more than a year,

I slept,

With you beneath my head.

Wherever I went,

Your little picture,

Was either,

In my hand,

Or in my pocket.

That's quite a long time in my book.

Bathing with blades

Brian was limping,

When they brought him back,

From the courtroom late last night.

As he rocked at the sink with no plug,

His coat tails,

His braces down by his side,

His sentence on the table,

And the bar-of-soap,

They had left him,

Embedded with scraps.

Wore a *white* T-shirt

I was pursued,

Into my class today,

With angry glares and the downcast eye.

Hasty phone calls were made,

Guards were waiting for me on the stairs.

The sneers of fellow in-mates,

Across the landing,

Foul language,

From appalled and high-class kitchen staff,

And the boorish unrefined,

Wearing only blue.

Well fucked-up

You,

Are well fucked up,

She said.

And believe me.

I'm an expert.

We grew up together,

And I know you, like the back of my hand,

A real live loser!

Still waters run deep

Eponymous hero of the great divide,

Whose boundless flame one flurried on a headwind,

Ask why the random raindrops crash,

On bearded temples,

Where the gilded traveller lutes,

Reluctant bellman of this sunless world,

Before the brooding winter slams its night,

In hymns forever to the flowering child,

Grey eminence of the fallen star,

Confined to flames of wine,

Where the eagle no longer calls the gushing blood-red sunset.

Unfeeling Captain of the thinking-heart,

Shall I tell you why the wheel no longer turns,

And boom-sails no longer bind the wind,

For long ships cindered in the cauldron of the stars,

No longer storm clouds gathered,

Now the bird has flown,

Though windless pools still smile and raise a sigh,

And echoes of a distant shore pull down the grains,

In wood-notes from this toll of acid skin,

To summer snow-men drifting in a line,

Landru is dead,

And nothing but a has-been…

Genny's yellow sucky-blanket

It was a wiry old thing,

Made from some kind of fleece,

With a hard bump along the edge,

Which we didn't like.

A soft fuzz of down,

Like gestures from the Sun,

Where we had been tugging,

When she sang our lullabies.

Black sheep-dog singing at the bottom of the stairs

Saturday afternoons at three,

Hot and steamy in the heat,

Door wide open to the street,

TV blaring…

I had no mouth-organ to excite him,

That barking-mad hound who was crooning.

If you don't like it,

You know what you can do.

Do you remember Karen Kenyon

A small boy,

Watching in the distance,

As you walked,

Your German shepherd to the park.

Who could run like the clappers if you smiled,

Who held you once,

Unblemished,

In his arms…

Seeing stars in Holker Street

It was dark I grant you,

And accidents will happen.

I didn't see it coming,

That fist from the left,

As we walked.

We were talking,

About Jimmy Greaves, Allan Gilzean, and Mike England,

When it landed,

Completely out-of-the-blue.

Out of nowhere.

What you should do son

My Dearest Son,

You are a great disappointment to me and you have brought shame upon all the family. You have only yourself to blame for where you have ended up. Please do whatever you are told and for once accept the advice you have been given. You are mentally ill and should be incarcerated in a hospital for the rest of your life instead of being cooked up in prison.

Love,

Mum x

Canon Fodder *Bird Dung*

"Hello folks! It is I, Canon Fodder here with you once again."

"How pleased I am to see you looking so well. The young thugs of this fine country make brilliant plant food. Here on the Western Front I am due to bless one of the tanks at dawn. The party will be in the mess on Monday evening.

I can think of no better sacrifice for a small overcrowded island."

Veronica

I wonder if she dreams,

In that High-chair of hers,

Of Poets and Princes,

Kissed by the light of the Moon.

And when she's silent in her place,

Words I try to whisper,

Silently,

And make believe,

She hears my ardent thoughts,

Within her mind.

If like a river to the haunting sea,

Each migrant wave upon a sunlit shore,

The dream,

In which I impulsed you long ago,

Through thorns and brambles,

Woken with a kiss...

Vistas of the world in vital colours,

Flood on by...

As day by day the blossom hidden from the star,

Bewildered in a maze,

I vex,

And strive to catch her gaze,

She smiles serene, and returns,

Ever to the changing screen. If while rocking on your dining-chair,

I caressed your hand as strangers do,

Perhaps, your heart would open like a rendered leaf,

Those bells darling,

You'd hear today from me...

More than the enemy we keep

If there's one thing that I know,

When I'm travelling home to you,

Through the heart-ache and the mayhem and the fog,

The world in which we live,

The body that we give,

Is just a passing shadow for the soul.

If you say that you have been,

In places rich in form,

If it's true,

there's no denying there will be pain.

But the sadness that I feel,

The hurt within these walls

It's just you,

And not your body,

Which I grieve…

You wander through the mist,

With the eyes that I have kissed,

But your body is just a shelter for your soul,

The dwelling that I know,

The you within this shell,

The one I love forever,

that's the most.

Garland of seared wood

Motionless you stand,

With a hint of salt,

Like a sentinel of Time with your felt-tipped sorrows,

Scrolls of spattered paint,

Scratching and piercing the wilderness,

Where a spider's web of colours,

Covers and rambles your nakedness.

Curtseys of brown swooning and swimming the silence,

Unarmed and frail,

Sinking into the earth…

The frost like jewels on a garment of green,

And the hand of the Moon,

like a branch of cinnamon,

Holding you,

Loving you,

The shivers down your spine,

You are really too small for me to rest in.

Being a wizard

Being a wizard,

As you know,

Gives me the power,

To come and go.

First you'll see me,

Then you won't,

In the sky,

Or flying north.

In your dreams I'll sit and talk,

Beside your bed or in your thoughts.

When you wake and take a look,

At the door or in your book.

You'll find me there,

Or in the air,

Turned into shade,

Or made of wood.

When all the stars come out tonight,

The Moon is bright,

For you my love.

Lee Rigby killer gets a taste for boot leather

By Rumplestiltskin | Published: December 11, 2015 | Edit

Another violent prisoner has been given a 'good' hiding by Officers working for the caring humane prison service, said the 'Ministry of Justice' today. Apparently there was a queue at the dentist's and the prisoner couldn't wait. Two of his teeth were accidentally removed during the procedure:

- All in the line of duty
- Working for your protection
- Refused to obey a command ("Tie that shoe-lace you BBN....!")

The box jelly man

By Sarin | Published: December 6, 2014 | Edit

I went to see the Box jelly man last night. He went over time.

After he was stung by five jelly fish many years ago he died and arose into heaven to talk to Jesus. He'd figured out a long time ago that if he could talk to God then God must be able to talk back. A wise man. If only he had listened to his mother's advice he would never have been such an atheist in the first place.

After being laid out in the morgue he awoke in a black void where he could only see the outline of his body. It was filled with evil spirits; people who had not obeyed the word of God or who had blasphemed against the Holy Ghost. They whispered things like "this is a dark and miserable place because we can't see anything. If only we hadn't been so wicked."

Soon after saying the **'Our Father'** a beam of light came down from heaven and took him up to God. Heaven was filled with refulgent light and the face of Jesus sent out silver beams of love which covered him in a sort of radio-active after glow. Jesus had hair like snow, just as it said in the bible.

Jesus asked if he would "like to return?" That's all he said.

The Box jelly man said that although heaven was a wonderful place full of happiness and joy he really wanted to return to earth.

Far better to live out his days here than in *Paradise*.

I walked to the front of the hall. He reached and shook my hand, still wiping away the tears from his eyes.

"Are you *born again?*" he asked with a sincere and expectant gaze.

NO THANKS!

Comments

I find this bordering on insulting. Bishop Desmond Tutu. December 2008.

ASBO'S CAN BE ORDERED ON-LINE BY ANYONE SEEKING TO IMPROVE THEIR MIND SET.

THEY COME IN A *RANGE OF COLOURS* AND CAN BE TAILOR-MADE AND CRAFTED <u>*BY THE EXPERT*</u> TO MEET YOUR NEEDS.

FOR A SMALL FEE SPELLS CAN BE PRODUCED TO HALT YOUR ENEMY IMMEDIATELY IN THEIR TRACKS OR MAKE THEM WAIT A WHILE UNTIL THEY SUDDENLY BURST INTO FLAMES.   **GB**

BUNDERCHOOK

Anti-Social Behaviour Order for:

General Leopoldo Fortunato Galtieri Castelli

dob July 15 1926

The following conditions must be implemented WITHOUT FURTHER DELAY:

1 You will refrain from electrocuting *Jorge Rafael Videla* or *Roberto Eduardo Viola*.

2 You will be punctual and keep your inform clean and your buttons gleaming.

3 You will not assassinate any member of the Government without consultation with Battalion 601.

4 Before kidnapping any member of the public you will liaise with the 11the Baronet of the Binns.

5 You will only meet behind closed doors.

6 You will be made a scapegoat.

*Failure to pacify your enemies may result in serious loss of prestige.

Most popular on You-Tube

POLICE HARASSMENT APPROVED BY PARLIAMENT

POLICE HARASSMENT APPROVED BY TORY
GOVERNMENT (4)

Police gang call in for further training on porn web-sites

SAD

BEEKEEPER SIGNS REGISTER ACCOMPANIED BY CHOIR OF
ANGELS

TWO BEE OR NOT TO BE

BEEKEEPER PURSUED BY SWARM OF GIANT BEES

FURTHER EXAMPLES OF POLICE HARASSMENT
SUPPORTED BY GOVERNMENT

Angry Hitchcock exposes nuisance bitch-cops

BORN AGAIN CHRISTIAN CULT

Police harassment of alleged Sex-offender

Police harassment of pensioner with Alzheimer's

Mafia hoods widen search for cami-knickers

Pinky and Perky learn how to dance

How to deal with persistent ass-wipes

With regard to statement (3) EXHIBIT LH8 from Louise H.

1 I did swear at Mr Yahman when he delivered the amendment outside my mother's home and I did react with
hostility. This was purely out of shock and indignation.

2 Even though I had moved away from *Bure Valley Zoo* months ago he still could not stop hounding me and in my opinion was still trying to brand me as something I am not.

3 I told him the truth; that the original injunction hearing which I did not attend was a lot of malicious lies from people who had nothing better to do.

4 My mother is a frail old lady who lost her husband a short time ago and is not in the best of health. It caused my mother and myself a lot of stress we could all do without.

5 As I have already written in my *letter to the Judge*, I did let myself down, but this sorry business has gone on for so long it is giving everyone a headache. It would make even a Saint swear!

6 Mr Yahman is deliberately trying to give me a bad name and seems to be only interested in my label.

7 In my opinion he deliberately came with the police to embarrass me in front of my new neighbours. I am just fed up of being harassed. This is all about labels.

8 **Mr Yahman was in no danger. For PC Scott to say that had he not been there I would have splattered Mr Yahman all over the concrete pavement is pure speculative nonsense, but what do you expect from someone predisposed to prejudice and with an IQ lower than his boot size.**

9 It is fair to say that I did react emotionally to the shock of having the police waiting for me when I came round the corner. It's no excuse, but I have been getting a lot of headaches due to stress.

10 I thought Mr Yahman was totally unjustified in bringing the police with him. When PC Scott said that had he not been there I would have reacted a lot worse is completely wrong. It is actually the other way round. Had the officer and the police car not been brought along I think I would have been a lot calmer and more civil.

I felt as if I was being victimized once more and that I am not being allowed to move on. Nearly eight years ago I contacted an ex partner when I had been told not to. I did not mean any harm and I was not trying to get back with her but have been getting harassed about it ever since. The neighbours were all told about my past before I went to live there making it very hard to settle down or be accepted.

NB I find it hard to understand what this incident has to do with the Application for an Injunction Amendment, unless it is to make me fit my stereo-type. I do not normally swear or use foul language, *unlike some of my accusers.* This is not the first time Mr Yahman has done the dirty on me. When Mr Didwell found a live bullet in the laundry some years ago the police were sent straight to my door even though I had nothing at all to do with it.

I believe the facts in this Statement are true and correct:
Signed: *Blunderchook*
Date: *April 1 1917*

*What about the numerous complaints of theft from the laundry and offensive language being added to my posters while I was there?
You claimed I had no evidence to prove who kept calling us names.
Let's face it Yahman.
You're a little shit and so are all your friends down at the Pig-Wagon.

How to deal with persistent snooping

The best way to deal with persistent Internet Snoops is to summon an entity which will cause them many a sleepless night until their final unexpurgated demise.

It will be like a presence continually watching over their shoulder. Like a hand held in abeyance as they bend to pick a piece of dropped litter on the edge of the platform. A steamroller trundling over their misshapen skull lying dead on the road.

COMMENTS

"For God's sake leave me in the Land of Nod," she hissed with loathing.

"But...but I'm a doctor!" he stuttered. "You've forgotten to take all your buttercup syrup."

The bungler flew like a bald bat out of hell back to the secret recesses of his unhallowed pit and fell into a melting mood. He shivered as if his useless existence was finished, breaking out into a cold unhealthy downpouring.

It looked as if he was floating in it. It was a dirty bird indeed that fouled its own nest.

Was this to be the culmination of 'Nosferatil's' cankered esse? He would surely be tried with a sanctified stake through his palpitating core, and final, unexpurgated *euthanasia*.

Head-hunters crunking in the *pantry*, entering their chamber through the trap-door, she stormed, panic stations, vain regret!

The irate *villagers* were gathering under the gloomy shadows of the bell tower...shambling behind the barrier reef..milkies!

Lanterns and shadows squiggled the dark-door as the alert stockman pursued the passageway for the evil manifestation.

A clarion call of yoiks oscillated through the entire house and into the dove-cote as he *copied a dead man* with the iron bolt carefully drawn.

Anybody there? Thunders of the Vatican! Her father examined the floor for a *poltergeist* disturbance but still they omitted to vex his dampened bridge.

Crazy as a garbage collector. Six feet under. Sold out of commission.

"Go back to bed!" the forces Chaplain pragmatically recommended. "Ghosts can't hurt you, only the living will!" Sleep safe my tortured love...

At the first cockcrow of dawn the morning blush of sunlight found his webbed feet hopping rapidly over pales.

192

"A typing error in your file!" yawned Stalker. "It should have read...'delayed a train,' for five minutes. I'll have it rectified at once."

"I advise you to accept their kind proposal!" urged the cantankerous mayor.

"Otherwise it's the sack, and you'll lose all your free travel." Wasn't that the Mason's grip they were both using?

F. considered the body of doctrine with reluctance. It was this final point which finally tipped the scales in their favour.

On his first day at the Terminus the *cider squeezers* searched for any reason they could to send him for an early bath. The *esprit de corps* turned the air blue with their Billingsgate banter.

Under the canopy *Robinson Crusoe* struggled to barber the platform sign as it swung in the Chinook. All good experience for a potential psychiatric nurse. But only F. seemed to realize that Rentagob was really a brown-nose. Gaffer! — hold his head above water...

At the *time capsule* in the distance the supervisor and his staff indulged in personalities as he blushed with obvious embarrassment. Various shades of *Pigmen* crept out of the woodwork during obtenebration it would seem. Tried to 'rise above his station.'

A member of the *S.S.* waited on the tarmac below him. Perhaps there was a cryptic code of practice which he had not twigged just yet. The *Afrikander* stared right through him as if he had just beamed from a foreign continent. He knew better than to force a direct contact with her though.

O'Flanagan had done his level best to block the Flasher's unpopular placement.

When the L.D.C. official had failed to implement his resolution he had corroborated the remainder of the *partisans* to send the deviant straight to Coventry. There was a hideous scar across his southern lip from a drunken brawl outside the *Golden cockerel* decades since.

224

The strange case of the fountain pen and the footprint

I raced along the wall and heard a hard thump as he jumped over the other side. Then I heard the swerve of a car as it skidded along the pavement. There was a splash near the harbour walls.

I was almost out of breath.

Just as I was about to give up I heard a loud shout. Footsteps echoed across the terrace.

A newspaper floated along on the wind.

I walked carefully up to the cliff edge and bent down to examine the grass. I stood up, but I couldn't see a damned thing. It was dark and a thin mist was blowing in from the shore. All I could see were a few lights glinting out at sea and the silhouette of Old Harry's rock way over to the west. I slammed the door of the model T Ford and returned along the path past the Tram lines. It was quiet as I walked up the steps apart from one little old lady with a walking stick who was just entering the lounge. A man with a tray met me in the foyer.

"Could I possibly make a private telephone call? It's a matter of life and death."

He ushered me into a side room and handed me the candlestick phone.

I told him my name and said that I required the Manager.

Pettigrew met me on the stairs.

"I need you to come with me down to the beach but first we need to check the rooms."

The Manager came towards me looking somewhat concerned.

"'Would you mind if I took a quick look at your *Register*?"

I flashed my ID and told him my name.

My finger skimmed down the list of names:

"Herbert Culpepper. Occupation: Fountain pen repairer...

May 3rd 1939. 1400hrs."

Pettigrew laughed.

"Can you describe him?"

We ascended the stairs and made our way to room nine.

The Manager unlocked the door and let us in.

"Police Inspector! He was last seen leaving the building at around half past eight this morning. He seemed in rather a hurry."

"Is that opium I can smell?" I placed the quill back in its holder.

"Golly. Isn't that a pick and shovel stood in the corner by the trouser press...?"

I walked over to the window where the half drawn curtain blew in the breeze and looked out onto the oil-lamp.   The bells of St Peters were just finishing.

A copy of 'The Tempest' lay open on the book shelf, with a postcard of Bournemouth pier on page thirty five.

"Check underneath the bed. There's something not quite right here."

Pettigrew pulled out a large brown suitcase from underneath the single bed and hoisted it up on the top.

"It weighs a bloody ton Sir!"

The case was covered in an assortment of labels: AMSTERDAM, EDINBURGH, BELFAST. Tunbridge Wells. Hotel Cremona, BOURNEMOUTH.

It was tied with a worn leather strap with the name '*Hugo Boss*' emblazoned on the buckle.

"Would you mind if I opened the case and examined its contents?" I looked up at the Manager. He nodded.

I sprung the lock and the hinges sprang up leaving the lid dangling in the air.

We all jumped with shock. The suitcase contained a large rock. That was all. We were both totally flummoxed.

A plain piece of rock in an old suitcase. How bizarre!

"'What shall we do?"

"Let's get down to the West beach as soon as we can."

I asked Pettigrew to bring a blanket from his room and we set off in haste.

We said goodbye to the Manager on St Michael's Road and made our way down to the beach past the pine clad slopes and sandy inlets.

Just as we rounded a small rock pool Pettigrew let out a sharp cry.

"What's that over there?" He pointed the beam of the torch ahead of us.

We both broke into a quick jog. Thirty yards or so away a body lay face down in the mush.

"The seagulls have certainly been busy tonight…" Pettigrew turned on his heel and screwed up his face.

I bent down to examine the body and removed a knife from between its fingers.

"Fallen, or *pushed*?" I scratched my head.

A thick bush of chalky coloured hair laced with particles of sand quaked in the draught.

I turned him gently over and replaced the dentures which had fallen by his side.

The tell-tale proliferation of sun-spots. The orange cravat.   Above it a flushed cheek of surprise. A polka-dot hanky in the top left hand corner pocket of his jacket. The odour Cologne. A red and yellow striped suit with brogues. A large flamboyant signet ring. The abnormally expanded right ear, hideously malformed and misshapen, with its payload of debris.

A huge Homburg with a peacock feather, and of course, strung to his monocle, of all things, a silver fountain pen, by Harrods.

I knelt down on the sand beside him to take a closer look and gazed up at Pettigrew, who was jotting down notes with great alacrity.

"Stratford Bobs! Notorious jewel thief and *bogus fountain-pen-restorer.* Fraudster, bigamist, and money-launderer. We have you at last!"

I threw up my arms in relief.

Pettigrew covered the body and made all the necessary arrangements while I returned back to the Hotel Cremona.

I asked the Manager if I could look over the room once more.

He turned the key in the lock.

There was the suitcase on the bed where we had left it.

A large shaving bowl stood on a small table near the writing desk.

There were some newspaper cuttings on the *chaise longue* along with a bottle of ink. Various hammers and assorted tripods surrounded the skirting board.

I walked over and lifted the archaic torso of stone in the case to see if there was anything on the other side.

We both arched over its contents. The slab of fossilized rock was dark brown in colour with a green patch in the middle. It could have been millions of years old: possibly Triassic. A carbuncle of molluscs gathered around the topmost edge. It wasn't an ordinary piece of rock at all but an extremely rare piece of natural history.

Right there in the centre was what

appeared to be *a human footprint*.

"How he found it is anybody's guess."

I picked up the phone to the British museum.

That's more than forty years ago now and I'm still not allowed to disclose its whereabouts...

My name: *Herbert Culpepper*.

BIOGRAPHY

Four major works of poetry:

Never let the dead Man cry (1996)
The bear who talked to Automobiles (2010)
Putting On Emily's shoes (2011)
Burning of the Scarlet Hearts (2012)

Born near Haworth, West Yorkshire, son of an English schoolteacher and Irish rebel.

Father a major sponsor of the Guinness Corporation and member of Sinn Fein.

Occasionally attended a reputable Catholic Grammar School.

Signalman, Art therapist, and Teacher of Sign-language.

Professional arm-wrestler.

Expert in counter-intelligence.

In 2007 was caught in possession of a Browning semi-automatic revolver.

Winner of the Koestler award for Literature.

Contender for the *Prix Goncourt*.

Winner of the Welsh Open poetry competition.

Author of the infamous 'THUNDERBUCK RAM.'

IF YOU REALLY LOVE HER

If you really love her
tell her that you love her,
do not let this vital moment pass,
do not wait until the moon is bright,
or you think she's of an equal heart!

If you really love her
tell her that you love her,
do not delay a second longer than you must,
do not turn away from this immortal yearning;
or fill your heart with tears of vain regret.

If you really love her
then tell her that you love her,
do not forsake this magic wonderland,
fly her beyond the peaks of all creation,
and make a bird of heaven overjoyed.

If you really love her,
then, tell her that you love her,
lay this gentle kiss upon her soul,
ask her to keep your promise safe,
until this sweetest blossom falls to land.

Like a conquering Vesuvius the crazy Flash erupted powerfully into her lap with hot spurts of sap...each particle of shakra more beautiful than the last. The girl cocained spellbound. She licked her lips and lapped up the waters drooling from the corners of her orifice where he wove his tantra.

While F. *holystoned* the trajectory with the material of her beret she curved away to the horizon. Having consumated their brief partnership she now carried a full cherry in the lull supervening the star chamber.

"Are you from Darlington?" she drolled. "Perhaps we'll meet on the campus."

What a wash-out. F. had burnt their britches in primary school. But it was no use crying over spilt cow's sip.

"'A mon destine, desormais mon delice,'" he told her, and slowly retired down the van to polish his philosopher's stone.

As her ankles wavered toward the barrier the high ranking official arrived to offer him a place with the troika. She walked with her eyes down to her toes.

The woman-dressed-in-black concurred with the guy as he settled in the comfort chair on their right and harmonised with the faith. Had the *nephillim* not been a corpuscle butch he may have stayed on for *After-eights.*

Her gaol-bird was handcuffed against the arch and had just been dragged to ablutions. F. noticed how pale she had become since her recent exit-pole. He engaged the other scantling in a discussion about ice-hockey until he could mince the hay while the sun shone hot. Fishy character? Cost him a fortune in bog-roll.

The captive insisted on making eyes over the table and airing her dirty linen in public. She was being ejected *back into care.* A holiday in the Jamaica blue would no doubt prove more salubrious than the slums of Soho, if she ever managed to elude their manacles.

The strange little man positioned himself a percentage forward of the Archbishop in his purple mantle.

299

Printed in Great Britain
by Amazon